Are you ready to start a fire?

MATCHBOOK

Forty-Day Faith Challenge
to Ignite Your Faith

Dr. Kim Mendoza

Matchbook

Publisher: Plainview LimeLite, LLC.
In Association with Blue Fire Faith
Plainview, Texas

www.kimmendoza.com

United States of America

Scriptures in this book were obtained
from Bible Gateway.
Holy Bible, New International Version®,
NIV® Copyright ©1973, 1978, 1984, 2011 by Biblica, Inc.®

Cover Design: Kimberlee R. Mendoza
Editorial Reader: LeeAnn Abrams
Structural Editor: Ashley Edlin, MFA

Some copyediting was completed by Google Gemini.

ISBN: 979-8-218-85498-0

DEDICATION

To Richard, Ethan, & Maya for always
challenging me in my own walk.

To my prayer partner Ashley Edlin
and to
Dr. Cindy McClenegan
& Dr. Karen Beth Strovas
for making the "call" that
brought me to my purpose.

Matchbook

"...He rewards those who earnestly seek him."

(Hebrews 11:6b)

⚡ THE CHALLENGE

This book is not just another devotional—it is a CHALLENGE. If you take the *Matchbook Challenge*, you are certain to grow in your faith. But—you'll need to be "all in."

So, what is the *Matchbook Challenge*?

For forty days, you will block out the world and lean into God. Often the Lord is unable to speak to us because there is so much "worldly noise." With this in mind, you will be asked to give up some distractions that hinder us from being immersed in His presence. These are the time thieves and disruptors of our thoughts.

As with any challenge, it won't be easy; it may stretch your "spiritual muscles" like never before. I liken it to a juice cleanse or a new healthy regimen, where you change your diet and go to the gym more. Continuing with that analogy, you will relinquish all "worldly junk food" and fill your time with "spiritually healthy alternatives." The more you feed your physical body nutritious food and exercise, the stronger it becomes—the soul is no different.

For the next forty days, I dare you to take this CHALLENGE. I believe your spiritual life WILL change. Who knows what God may do with and through you?

I have completed this challenge with people of all ages, and what happens on the other side of it is amazing. People are called into full-time ministry. Miracles happen. Torn relationships are restored. But most of all, everyone (who completes it) always feels closer to God.

If you're ready to be on FIRE for Jesus, then you have to give in and let go of everything. The Holy Spirit is a gentleman and won't work in your life any more than you allow Him. So, are you willing to do all it takes to ignite your faith?

Are you ready to STRIKE THE MATCH?

If you draw near to God, He will draw near to you
(James 4:8).

Author's Tip: *Many statements are backed up by scripture. Consider looking in the footer for additional scriptures to read on the various topics.*

WHAT YOU WILL NEED:
- A journal & pen
- A Bible
- Optional (but recommended): A prayer partner
- A willingness and commitment

A METHOD FOR PRAYER:

Jesus tells his disciples to **TARRY** *in Jerusalem until they received the power from God.* [1]

T—Thank God for Who He Is

A—Ask for forgiveness

R—Remember other's needs

R—Request those things you need

Y—Yield and listen to what God has for you

Prayer is not an appointment. Prayer is a lifestyle.

---

[1] Luke 24:49

For supplemental sermons, check out
@BlueFireFaith on YouTube.

STEPS TO STARTING A FIRE

I. Clearing Out a Space

(SURRENDER & SUBMIT)

Day 1—Removing the Debris

Day 2—Tossing the Leftovers

Day 3—Accepting the Cost

Day 4—Relinquishing the Staff

Day 5—Sifting the Ash

Day 6—Trusting the Ranger

Day 7—Discarding the Soot

Day 8—Eliminating the Needles

II. Building a Foundation

(PRAYER & THE WORD)

Day 9— Reading the Safety Manual

Day 10— Setting the Tinder

Day 11— Pitching the Wet Wood

Day 12— Igniting the Toxic Branch

Day 13— Striking with Focus

Day 14—Listening to Smokey

Day 15— Sitting around the Ring

Day 16—Nursing the Ember

V. **Fanning the Flames**

(*PREPARE & SHARE*)

DR. KIM MENDOZA

PART I

CLEARING OUT A SPACE

"SURRENDER & SUBMIT"

To build a fire, it is essential to make a safe place for it to grow. There are rules to creating this space. First and foremost, the area has to be free of debris. Failing to complete this step can turn a useful fire into a destructive force.

In the case of this challenge, you will need to clean out the "debris" in your life through *surrender*. These first eight days of the challenge will likely be the hardest and most uncomfortable, as they will focus on purging the "comforts" that hinder your spiritual walk.

If you are willing to embrace it this challenge, it will encourage you to lean into God and block out the world. I like how Peter states it: "Therefore, since Christ suffered in his body, arm yourselves also with the same attitude, because whoever suffers in the body is done with sin." [2] Scripture also mentions cleaning away the "dross" several times in conjunction with purifying oneself. [3]

So, as you start this challenge, it is important to understand that the "clearing of the dross" is necessary if you want your FIRE to ignite and burn bright!

---

[2] I Peter 4:1
[3] Proverbs 25:4; Isaiah 1:16

"Fire doesn't fall
on empty alters.
There has to be a sacrifice
on the altar
for the fire to fall."

(Tommy Tenney, Author of God Chasers)

∴ **DAY 1** ∴

Removing the Debris

Finally, brothers and sisters,
whatever is TRUE, whatever is NOBLE,
whatever is RIGHT, whatever is PURE,
whatever is LOVELY, whatever is ADMIRABLE—
if anything is EXCELLENT or PRAISEWORTHY—
think about such things.
(Philippians 4:8, NIV)

"Whatever you put into your mind
becomes part of the total you"
(Zig Ziglar, Speaker, 1926).

DAILY READING:
Matthew 10:38-39; 16:26; Exodus 20:3

DAILY THOUGHT:
Before even starting a fire, we need to remove the debris—the waste, trash, junk—that will be in the way.

What would happen if all we ever ate was chips and cookies? How long before we started to feel sick? According to health experts, eating this way would greatly increase our risk of obesity and chronic disease, including diabetes, cancer, and ultimately, death.[4] The same can be said about what we "feed" our souls. If we only devour "worldly" entertainment, how long until our spiritual life suffers?

As mentioned, this challenge will feel like a "spiritual diet." But to be successful, you will need to cut things out of your life that make you spiritually unhealthy. You may be working "spiritual muscles" you're not used to working. In return, you will be eating the *Bread of Life*[5] and drinking *Living Water.*[6] Eventually, you will feel better and desire healthier things for your soul. This challenge will not always be easy. If you mess up one day, just get back on track the next day.

The first time I led a group through this challenge, one of the men said he couldn't "give up sports." I said, "Then that's exactly what you should give up." He replied, "I'm sorry, I just can't." My response was

---

[4] Brissette, C. (2018). This is your body on fast food. *The Washington Post.*
[5] John 6:35
[6] John 4:10

simple: "If you can't give it to God for forty days, you should ask yourself, *why*?"

Those things we cannot give up for Jesus become mini "gods" in our lives. We are called to be fully surrendered. Nothing should be more important than our Savior as we are directed to "put our minds on things above."[7] This does not mean we never get to participate in fun activities; it means there shouldn't be anything that we cannot give up—especially, if and when God asks us to.

So, what is "junk food" to the soul? Anything of this world that does not point you to God. It doesn't always mean it is a sin, but it is likely a distraction. Examples of this might be *television, social media, Unhealthy Habits* (e.g. smoking, drinking, illegal drugs, gluttony, or too much caffeine), or *Distracting Hobbies* (e.g. sports, shopping, gaming, excessive exercise, or reading.) These will be different for everyone. You might ask, "How can these be 'junk food?' Aren't things like reading good for us?" Of course, but let me explain.

DAILY STORY:

---

[7] Colossians 3:2

I *love* to read. I usually read three books at a time. But there are times I would rather read my *recreational* books than read the Bible. That's when it becomes a distraction. In the past, fiction *was* "junk food." As I edited this book, I felt called to complete the challenge again. This time, my "junk food" was YouTube. It was feeding my soul in a negative way, and I felt like God said to give it up for 40 days.

I can't dictate what your "junk food" will be. That is between you and God to decide. If you're hoping God won't ask you to give something up... I'd start there.

REFLECTION:

Read the scriptures listed above, then reflect on them below. Pick out keywords, verses, and themes. Write down how those might apply to your life. Admit if there are areas where you struggle. The more honest you are about where you are at, the more quickly God can begin a good work in you.

Ask yourself, what are you feeding your soul? Spiritual junk food or healthy substance? What should you probably get rid of? Could you do it for 40 days? If not, write down in your journal why or why not.

_____

_____

_____

_____

_____

_____

_____

_____

_____

_____

_____

_____

PRAYER:

Lord, as I start this journey, reveal those things in my life that are in the way. Give me the strength to get rid of them and find peace without them. Help me complete this journey and find a burning passion for the Word of God and prayer. Amen.

WRITE YOUR OWN PRAYER:

_____

_____

_____

_____

_____

_____

_____

_____

_____

_____

_____

_____

_____

TODAY'S CHALLENGE: Your challenge is to give up one thing for the next forty days. Examples: *Videos, Games, Sports, Music, Social Media, Caffeine, Sugar, Shopping*, etc. Only you know what it is.

🔥 **DAY 2** 🔥

Tossing the Leftovers

Honor the LORD with your wealth,
with the first fruits of all your crops;
then your barns will be filled to overflowing,
and your vats will brim over with new wine.
(Proverbs 3:9-10, NIV)

"In our 24-hour day,
2 hours and 40 minutes (10%) do not belong to us."
(Origination Unknown)

DAILY READING:

Nehemiah 10:28-39; James 1:16-18; Malachi 3:10

DAILY THOUGHT:

Sometimes former campers have left behind trash in the fire pit. Before we can start our fire, we have to get rid of the *leftovers*.

I apologize in advance if you have read a book or heard a sermon where I share the following illustration, but I cannot think of a better way to make my point.

Imagine the King of England is coming to your home tonight. What would you serve him? Will you pull out your best china and crystal or use paper plates and red plastic cups? Would you hire a caterer or cook it yourself with whatever is in the cupboards? Would you serve steak and salmon, or pull out the leftovers from the night before?

We follow the *King of Kings*. He is in our house every night. So, why do we often serve Him the least of ourselves? Why do we give Him our stale leftovers instead of the highest quality of our time? Why do we *squeeze* Him into our schedules, instead of making Him *rule* our schedules?

DAILY STORY:

The first time I heard of "first fruits" was at the Annual Faith Chapel Women's Retreat. The women's pastor read Leviticus 23:9-14. She said, "We need to give God the first of ourselves, not what is left over. That means starting your day with God, not when you're falling asleep."[8] It was a new concept, and it struck home. I thought, *what would I do if someone important were to come to my home?*

The King of the Universe desires to spend time with us. He wants our undivided attention, and He is worthy of both. He deserves the finest part of us. So, ask yourself, are you giving the King of the Universe an elegant experience or just your surplus scraps?

---

[8] Meek, K. (2009), Faith Chapel Woman's Retreat.

REFLECTION:

Read the scriptures listed above, then reflect on them below. Pick out keywords, verses, and themes. Write down how those might apply to your life.

Ask yourself, what are my "fruits," and what would be the <u>first</u> of those fruits? When you look at the scriptures today, what are the various life choices spelled out for the Levites? How might that apply to your life?

_____

_____

_____

_____

_____

_____

_____

_____

_____

_____

_____

_____

_____

Matchbook

_____

_____

_____

_____

_____

_____

_____

_____

_____

_____

_____

_____

_____

_____

_____

_____

_____

_____

_____

_____

_____

PRAYER:

Dear Lord, forgive me for not giving you the utmost quality of my time and energy. Help me to always offer you the best of my heart, soul, and time. Amen.

WRITE YOUR OWN PRAYER:

_____

_____

_____

_____

_____

_____

_____

_____

_____

_____

_____

_____

_____

_____

_____

TODAY'S CHALLENGE: I challenge you to find at least one hour a day to pray. If your attention span suffers, this could be split up into 2-4 segments but imagine what God could accomplish in you, if you offered Him more quality time.

♨ DAY 3 ♨

Accepting the Cost

"Whoever wants to be my disciple
must deny themselves and
take up their cross and follow me."
(Matthew 16:24, NIV)

"There are no levels of surrender.
Either we surrender or we don't"
(Bob Sorge, Author of *Secrets of the Secret Place*).

DAILY READING:

Genesis 22:1-18; Romans 12:1-8

DAILY THOUGHT:

Having grown up with a single mom, I was taught to always buy the cheapest products. This notion frustrates my family, proving time and again that cheap products equal *low quality*. The failure of these purchases has become a running joke in our home. When writing this devotional, I asked Google: "What happens if I bought a cheap fire pit?" It wrote instability, critical safety concerns, and a guaranteed short lifespan (of the fire pit, not me). In other words, a bad outcome. Though it would pain me to see big dollars spent for a serious investment like a fire pit, I would have to surrender the purchase decision to someone else.

Surrender is not a word many of us like. But the truth is, if we do not surrender to God, our Christian walk can become unstable, and our fire will not burn bright. We are called to surrender our lives to God completely, 100%, holding nothing back.[9] We cannot hold tight to a part of ourselves and expect He will work in us.[10] He longs for more than a fraction—He requires all of us.

Which brings me to the point for this week—The price of salvation should cost us everything.[11] When we ask

---

[9] Romans 12:1-2
[10] Revelation 3:16
[11] Romans 12:2

Jesus into our lives, we indicate that we no longer want to live as we did before. Instead, we surrender to Him and trust Him with our daily walk, our finances, our decisions, our worries, and our families.

It is my assumption that a lot of Christians do not fully grasp what happened at Calvary. They *know* the story of Jesus' crucifixion, but how often do they let that *fully* sink in? As you go through this list below, take a moment to reflect on your own emotional reaction. Imagine each of these events happening *to you*, all in one night.

1. **REJECTED—Jesus was betrayed by His good friend,**[12] **denied by another friend,**[13] **abandoned by all His other friends,**[14] **and His "church" demanded His death.**[15]

   Jesus lived with Judas for three years. He loved him. Have you ever been betrayed by someone you care about? It cuts deep. In addition, Peter denied that

   ---

   [12] Matthew 26:49
   [13] Matthew 26:69-75
   [14] Mark 14:50
   [15] Matthew 27:22-27

he ever knew Jesus, and all His friends ran away. None of them were there to stand in His corner.

Second, the Jews were God's people, and yet, they were the ones fixated on killing His Son. Imagine if your church or social group insisted on your murder. It's hard to even fathom.

2. HUMILIATED—Endured Public Shaming

Jesus' crucifixion would have been humiliating. This respected Rabbi was now stripped of all His clothes,[16] while people hurled insults at Him. This must have been horrifying.

It should also be mentioned, for Jewish people, a person who dies on a tree was cursed by God.[17] So, beyond the social shaming, there would have been religious shaming, as well.

3. TORMENTED—The Romans beat Jesus until He was unrecognizable[18] and then made Him carry His own cross.[19]

---

[16] John 19:23
[17] Deuteronomy 21:22-23
[18] Isaiah 52:14; John 19:1
[19] John 19:17

First, a crown of thorns was placed on His head, and I doubt they set it on gently.[20] If I get one splinter, I'm upset.

Then, they whipped His bare body 39 times, to the point He no longer looked like Himself. The reason the flogging was so bad, was the Romans used scourge whips called "scorpions" (not a "cat of nine tails"), because the strands had metal balls and sharp bones attached to the ends.[21] Each lash would have taken a chunk of flesh with it, leaving Jesus, as one journal said, "bowels and bones."[22] This should introduce a deeper depth to the scripture, "by His stripes we are healed."[23]

Jesus had little skin left on His body. He'd lost a lot of blood, so He would have been weak. Most likely, He was close to death, yet, He had to walk a third of a mile, up a hill, with a heavy splintered beam scratching at His open sores. I don't know if you're like me, but when I get hurt, I just want to crawl into bed and stay there.

---

[20] Matthew 27:29

[21] King, K. (n.d.). Three Thirty Ministries

[22] Nicolotti, A. (2017). Journal for the study of the historical Jesus.

[23] I Peter 2:24

4. IMPALED—The Romans hammered nails into His body.[24]

The guards took long nails and struck them into His hands and feet. Ponder that for a moment. Have you ever stepped on a nail, a tack, or glass? I need to get it out to stop the hurting. But Jesus not only had to leave them in but hang from them. Adding to the trauma, they would have severed nerves, caused massive tissue damage, and damaged bone. Each brutal encounter would have been agonizing by itself. All of these at once is unfathomable.

5. FORSAKEN—The Father abandoned Jesus.[25]

More agonizing than the physical pain was the moment Jesus' eternal companion turned his back on Him. We can't even begin to fathom eternity, but we know the Godhead had always been One. For the first time in all existence, Jesus was truly and completely alone—a profound abandonment that eclipses any human farewell.

6. MURDERED—He was innocent yet killed.[26]

---

[24] John 20:25-27
[25] Matthew 27:46
[26] Matthew 35:44

Have you ever been accused of something you did not do? Jesus was innocent. Pilate and his wife said so themselves, but the religious leaders still demanded His execution.[27] This, by definition, is murder.

7. EXECUTED—He died on a cross.[28]

Dying by crucifixion was one of the most excruciating and humiliating ways to die. It was not uncommon for birds and bugs to pick at the flesh of the dying.[29] Jim Caviezel (an actor who played Jesus) said, he dislocated a shoulder carrying the cross, almost bit his tongue off, was struck by lightning while hanging on the cross, had pneumonia and hypothermia, and had to endure two heart surgeries because of it.[30] And he was just acting in the role. In truth, crucifixion was a slow death by asphyxiation. As their strength failed, the victims became too weak to push up, and so they slowly suffocated.

Knowing all of this, how can anyone think it is okay to just give Jesus a portion of time, money, or commitment? If even one of those seven things above

---

[27] John 19:4-7
[28] Matthew 27:44
[29] Marina, M. (2023). [History].
[30] Caviezel, J. (2024). "I was struck by lightning." TBN.

happened to us, we'd be shaken to our core. But Jesus, who could have ended the suffering with a mere thought, endured the humiliation and anguish (both physically and mentally) for us with humility and love. This debt can never be repaid; therefore, everyone on this planet owes Jesus everything and more.

This week, you're reading about Abraham's ultimate sacrifice—his son. (God did not ask anything of Abraham that He wouldn't do Himself.) Isaac was *everything* to Abraham. He waited so long for his "miracle" boy. But God needed to know if Abraham could truly offer his most prized possession. The demonstration of this is key to success in our spiritual lives. We must put our entire lives on the altar. The beautiful and recurring message in scripture is that whenever God took something away, He gave it back better than before beyond human comprehension.[31] Just look at Job's life. The Bible states, "The LORD blessed the latter part of Job's life more than the first."[32]

---

[31] Haggai 2:9; Joel 2:25; I Corinthians 2:9; Isaiah 64:4
[32] Job 42:12

DAILY STORY:

A while back, the church I worked for asked the staff to pray each day. So, I spent thirty minutes at the altar each morning. God asked me to surrender my life. Not one part—but all. So, I put my ministry, my job, my house, my car, my family, my future...all of it on the altar. Then, He took away my ministry, my job, my house, my car, and my future plans within weeks of that prayer. I considered crawling into the fetal position and bawling, "How could you God?" But I didn't. I prayed harder. And God gave me back a ministry, a house, a car, a better job, and my purpose that I am still walking in today.

Surrender *may* mean losing something at first, but God doesn't take these things to be cruel. He does it to make us the best versions of ourselves. If God has asked you to give something up, it will bring you to a better place, and a better you. So, lay it down. Empty yourself. Surrender. Your effort will be a blessing on the other side.

REFLECTION:

Read the scriptures listed above, then reflect on them below. Pick out keywords, verses, and themes. Write down how those might apply to your life.

Reflect on the crucifixion account above. What is going through your mind. Be specific.

_____

_____

_____

_____

_____

_____

_____

_____

_____

_____

_____

_____

_____

_____

_____

_____

PRAYER:

Dear Jesus, please forgive me for anything that I am holding onto that you have specifically asked for me to get rid of. Give me the strength to surrender all to you. Amen.

WRITE YOUR OWN PRAYER:

_____

_____

_____

_____

_____

_____

_____

_____

_____

_____

_____

_____

_____

_____

TODAY'S CHALLENGE: Is there anything you are still not willing to give up? If so, my challenge to you today is to see if you can surrender and place that "thing" on the altar.

🔥 DAY 4 🔥

Relinquishing the Staff

Humble yourselves, therefore,
under God's mighty hand,
that He may lift you in due time.
(I Peter 5:6, NIV)

"Let God have your life;
He can do more with it than you can"
(D.L. Moody, Evangelist, 19th Century).

DAILY READING:

James 4; Luke 6:46-47

DAILY THOUGHT:

A *fire staff* is used to tend a fire. Whoever holds it is in charge of keeping it going. Yesterday, we talked about surrender (dropping it, no matter the cost). Now that we are surrendered, we need to submit to God's will.

Surrender is "letting go," but *submission* is the "letting God."

In war, when a platoon loses, they put up their hands and say, "We surrender," but surrender does not mean they have fully submitted. They could go on a hunger strike, refuse to answer questions, or even try to escape. Being "surrendered" is not the same as being "submitted." That stubbornness can often be painful and become one's downfall. Once we submit, that's when our lives begin to make sense.

In our society, a lot of people dislike the word "submit." It gives someone else the power to call the shots in one's life. And yes, that is exactly what submitting to God means. We allow Him to move into the driver's seat. There is an element of trust that comes with submission. It is the belief that God has the utmost intentions in mind and will take us on the best path.

Remember, this is a challenge, not a devotional. I said it would not be easy. I have taken this challenge four times now. Each time, it gets easier, but it is never *easy.* No challenge ever is. But to take our relationship with Jesus Christ to the next level, we have to stop fighting Him and say two simple words, "Yes, Lord." God's purpose may not always make sense to us, but it will *always* be the best path for us. Trust Him fully and agree to do whatever He asks of you. These forty days will challenge you to rest in God's grace and faithfulness. Your understanding of God grows in direct proportion to your submission to His will. Surrender and submission are foundational to a strong relationship with the Lord. You cannot have one foot in the world and one foot on the altar. There are many scriptures that tell you to choose a side.[33] As scripture states: Choose for yourselves this day, whom you will serve.[34]

DAILY STORY:

A lot of "modern" women choose to leave the word "submit" out of their wedding vows. Though I may believe in women's rights, I also believe in the biblical order of the home. So, when I got married, I agreed to

---

[33] Matthew 6:24; Revelation 3:16; Luke 6:46
[34] Joshua 24:15

submit to my husband. My husband has only said a few times in our marriage, "No." When he said it, I lifted my hands up, shrugged, and said, "Okay, that's between you and God." I figure, he'll have to answer for that decision, not me. (For the ladies, it is actually freeing, not stifling.)

When we submit to God, we get to do the same thing. We can lift our hands, shrug, and say, "Okay God, it's all yours." How freeing is that? No more burden. Are you ready to submit to God, even if it may be outside your comfort zone? Are you willing to submit your time, your resources, and your family? Fully trusting Him with all that you are, all that you have, and all that you will become—is freedom. "So, if the Son sets you free, you will be free indeed."[35]

---

[35] John 8:36

REFLECTION:

Read the scriptures listed above, then reflect on them below. Pick out keywords, verses, and themes. Write down how those might apply to your life.

Make a plan. Schedule a time. Find a place. Make God a priority. Submit your life to Him.

_____

_____

_____

_____

_____

_____

_____

_____

_____

_____

_____

_____

_____

_____

_____

_____

_____

_____

_____

_____

_____

_____

_____

_____

_____

_____

_____

_____

_____

_____

_____

_____

_____

_____

PRAYER:

Dear Lord, help me submit to your will, fully trusting you with my journey. Amen.

WRITE YOUR OWN PRAYER:

_____

_____

_____

_____

_____

_____

_____

_____

_____

_____

_____

_____

_____

_____

TODAY'S CHALLENGE: God puts things on our hearts all the time. Often, we are afraid, or it goes against our own plans. My challenge to you today is to just say, "Yes, Lord." You don't have to have it all figured out to step into His will.

᭟ **DAY 5** ᭟

Sifting the Ash

It is for freedom that Christ has set us free.
Stand firm, then, and do not let yourselves
be burdened again by a yoke of slavery.
(Galatians 5:1, NIV)

"God sees us with the eyes of a Father.
He sees our defects, errors,
and blemishes. But He also sees our value"
(Max Lucado, Author & Speaker).

DAILY READING:

John 8:3-11; I Peter 2:9-12

DAILY THOUGHT:

Before starting a fire, it is important to sift the ash.
Though some ash is great as a foundation, talcum-like

ash can actually choke out the fire, as can any stray sand, soil, or impurities.

Yesterday, we talked about submission. That was the first step to freedom. But often, we may sift out the physical but still embrace the mental or spiritual. We become great at shoving our pasts into the shadowy corners of our mind. We use the world's commotion as a buffer, hoping to control the darkness and keep it hidden. But often, as people work through this challenge, their pasts begin to resurface—old insecurities, painful offenses, and bruised relationships. Fearful of what revealing them might mean, we might be tempted to thrust them back into the closet and lock the door.

Let me challenge you not to do that. Christ offers to clean out any old wounds and truly set us free.[36] We need to face our past hurts, insecurities, or thoughts. As Paul wrote, "For freedom Christ has set us free; stand firm therefore, and do not submit again to a yoke

---

[36] John 8:36

of slavery."[37] By not allowing Jesus to wipe that stuff away, we are still in bondage.

DAILY STORY:

I had a strange and divided childhood. My mother was a devout Christian, but my biological father was an agnostic addict. Many horrible things happened to me in my formative years, and in addition, in the U.S. Army, I experienced some horrible things. When I allow my past to linger, it causes havoc on my sleep, my treatment of others, and how I talk to Jesus. But, when I let God remove the pain, the hurts, and the past memories, everything changes. I recognize those events no longer define me or have power over me. I start to possess peace, acquire better sleep, and exhibit more joy.

Our identity isn't rooted in our past or present. We should not be defined by our relationships, the careers we choose, or the errors we've made. Our definition should come from God alone—who He says we are. We are forgiven. We are sons and daughters of the

---

[37] Galatians 5:1

King. We are royalty. If you are saved, you are no longer dead in your sin. You are a new creation and your past is gone. [38] You no longer live in old convictions, so hold your head high, and start walking in your *new* life. I know, we Christians "say" this. We may even believe it. But how many of us actually walk in it?

We must not let our past be hidden anymore. Even if it kicks and screams all the way, drag that ugly darkness into the light, where it can no longer dwell in our hearts. If you hide it, the enemy (I refuse to say *his* name) wins. But once you share your past, and find redemption from it, then God gets the glory. I have found the more I share, the more I am able to help someone else. Don't be ashamed. Be free. Share your testimony.

---

[38] II Corinthians 5:17

REFLECTION:

Read the scriptures listed above, then reflect on them below. Pick out keywords, verses, and themes. Write down how those might apply to your life.

Write down a label or situation you are holding onto. Then write down the opposite of that. Give yourself a brand-new one.

_____

_____

_____

_____

_____

_____

_____

_____

_____

_____

_____

_____

_____

_____

_____

_____

_____

_____

_____

_____

_____

_____

_____

_____

_____

_____

_____

_____

_____

_____

_____

_____

_____

_____

_____

_____

PRAYER:

Dear Lord, forgive me, free me, and help me walk in that freedom. Amen.

WRITE YOUR OWN PRAYER:

_____

_____

_____

_____

_____

_____

_____

_____

_____

_____

_____

_____

_____

_____

TODAY'S CHALLENGE: I challenge you, if you haven't yet, to write out your testimony. Then, sometime this week, share it with someone else.

🔥 **DAY 6** 🔥

Trusting the "Ranger"

Do everything without grumbling or arguing.
(Philippians 2:14, NIV)

"I hate to see complacency prevail in our lives when
it's so directly contrary to the teaching of Christ"
(Attributed to Former President Jimmy Carter).

DAILY READING:

*Joshua 6:1-5; Numbers 14:26-35; Psalm 106;
Philippians 2:14-16*

DAILY THOUGHT:

My stepdad was once a forest ranger. If I was going to
have anyone help me build a fire, it would be him. A
forest ranger is skilled at fire safety. If he told me to do
something, I wouldn't argue. I wouldn't complain. I
would just do it—because he would know best—he's
the expert.

In this scenario, God is the Forest Ranger. He is telling us how to live. How to be safe. What it will take to be on fire for Him. Often, He has us do something or be somewhere we don't want to go. We complain. Complaining is a sign of inaction. It diminishes who God is and what He might do. Rather than asking... "God, while I'm here in this place, what would You like me to learn from it?" ...we say, "I don't like where You put me." This indicates, there is a lack of trust.

The path from Egypt to Israel was only 1,500 miles (that's like walking from New York to Colorado). It should have only taken them eleven days to travel that distance. So, why did the Israelites, God's chosen people, get stuck wandering in the desert for *forty* years? The answer is simple. Instead of obeying, they were complaining.

It's natural to have concerns and ask God for more. But instead of complaining about our circumstances, we can learn to trust Him. If we don't, we too could be left to wander in the desert.

When the Israelites stopped complaining, God gave them Jericho. There is an important statement God made in Joshua 6:2, "See! I have given Jericho into your hand..." Why is this important? Because the Israelites had not marched around Jericho yet, and the walls still stood. Yet, God states, "I *have given*," not "I *will give*." In God's eyes, they had already won the city.

This past tense exchange should tell us a lot. Instead of complaining about the situation, we should thank God for what He has done and what He will do. The Bible states that we are to give thanks in all situations, for this is *God's will*, which tells me, we cannot expect God to show more of His plan for our lives, when we won't even obey the first part of His will.[39]

It takes realigning our thinking, trusting God, and obeying Him. Maybe you dislike your job or a co-worker. Praise God that you have a job (as many do not) and for the future He is preparing you for. Maybe your marriage is in shambles. Pray for your spouse (even if you want to deck him or her) and praise God

---

[39] I Thessalonians 5:18

for wisdom and strength. Maybe your kids are a wreck. Praise God that you have kids (some women are barren) and remember, God loves and cares for them, too. Maybe you are barren, praise God for His grace and love, and to show you other ways to be a mother to the many children in this world who have nobody.

I understand all of this is a challenge. Our problems are real. They hurt. They confuse. They are scary. They are frustrating. But in reality, complaining won't make the problem go away, and often, we feel worse. If, instead, we praise God and trust He is at work even when we can't see it, we begin to feel better, and our faith grows.

Now, what if God doesn't change our situation? We still must operate in faith. Scripture mentions that Paul needed healing and he prayed at least three times, where God responded, "My grace is sufficient for you, for My power is made perfect in weakness." [40] Sometimes, we pray and pray, and it seems God doesn't hear us. Let me assure you, He always hears

---

[40] II Corinthians 12:19

us.[41] But His purpose will be fulfilled in His way and time.[42] Some believe that Paul's bad eyesight was a reminder of how much God had forgiven him. David's running from Saul allowed him to show humility and respect for God in a powerful way, which would later make him a great king. Shadrach, Meshach, and Abednego had to go into the fire, but they were not alone.[43] Daniel had to go into the lion's den, so that a King could believe in God.[44]

DAILY STORY:

I personally am walking through a health issue, and I too have prayed and prayed for healing. One day, while I was once again praying, my eyes were opened to the blessing. The health issue has allowed me to slow down and spend more time with my Creator. In truth, I am able to write this book, because of moments like these.

---

[41] I John 5:15
[42] Romans 8:28; Isaiah 46:10
[43] Daniel 3
[44] Daniel 6:16-23

No matter where you are, or what you are doing, we are called to praise Him. [45] Praise Him in the best moments of life but also praise Him in the fire.

---

[45] Psalm 150:6

REFLECTION:

Read the scriptures listed above, then reflect on them below. Pick out keywords, verses, and themes. Write down how those might apply to your life.

Write down different situations, people, or things that you complain about. Then reflect on ways you can turn those things over to God.

_____

_____

_____

_____

_____

_____

_____

_____

_____

_____

_____

_____

_____

_____

_____

_____

_____

_____

_____

_____

_____

_____

_____

_____

_____

_____

_____

_____

_____

_____

_____

_____

_____

_____

_____

PRAYER:

Lord, help me to have a good attitude with the circumstances around me. Please help me to praise you in all circumstances, rather than complain. Amen.

WRITE YOUR OWN PRAYER:

_____

_____

_____

_____

_____

_____

_____

_____

_____

_____

_____

_____

_____

_____

_____

TODAY'S CHALLENGE: I challenge you today to pray earnestly for the leadership, the person (or people), or the situation that has become an annoyance. Don't just pray that things will be better for you...but pray that God will work on the organization, person, or situation.

⚶ **DAY 7** ⚶

Discarding the Soot

Be kind and compassionate to one another,
forgiving each other,
just as in Christ God forgave you.
(Ephesians 4:32, NIV).

"Forgive others, not because
they deserve forgiveness,
but because you deserve peace."
(Jonathan Lockwood Huie, Author)

DAILY READING:

Mark 11:25; Matthew 5:22-24; 18:21-22

DAILY THOUGHT:

Unforgiveness becomes like icky black soot to our heart. It can keep us bitter and unable to love as we should. Forgiveness is hard. Both directions. It is hard to do it when someone has wronged us, and it is hard to accept when God gives it to us freely. But both are equally important. First, let's address Jesus' forgiveness. The Bible states that when we are saved, we are free indeed,[46] and there is no condemnation for those who love the Lord. The Bible also states that once He forgives us, He forgets.[47] The only time the Lord knows about our sins is when we remind Him. So, we need to let that stuff go and know we are forgiven.

Now, let's look at forgiving others. We sometimes say, "I'll forgive, but I'm not going to forget." That is not forgiveness that mirrors God's example. Could you imagine if Jesus said that to us? No! When Christ forgives us, He releases it. We need to do the same. "For I will forgive their wickedness and will remember their sins no more."[48] In addition, we have orders. Jesus tells us to forgive seventy times seven.[49] We are called to forgive because He first forgave us. On a more practical level, if we do not forgive, then the

---

[46] John 8:36; Romans 8:1
[47] Isaiah 43:25
[48] Hebrews 8:12
[49] Matthew 18:21-22

person continues to hurt us. That person has likely moved on, but we are still being punished.

We are called to love. If we have unforgiveness in our hearts, we can't truly love that person. Additionally, we are giving them power in our lives, and the only one who should have power like that... is Jesus. We need to forgive—*and* forget. One of the verses you will read today suggests you need to lay your sacrifice at the altar and reconcile with your brother. Only then can we experience the true gift of God. This challenging journey you are on will not be as successful if you hold a grudge. (Now, a quick note: Forgiving and forgetting doesn't mean you need to "hang out with them." Some people are toxic. We can forgive, forget, and send them lovingly on their way.)

DAILY STORY:

During the last time I did this challenge, God revealed a deep bitterness I had inside. It was a heavy weight that made me snap at people. But the Holy Spirit allowed me to release it. I found new joy. And I'm not the only one. Another lady had lost three family members, one suddenly, one murdered, and one by suicide. She held bitterness towards God for decades. After taking this challenge, she too released and found the joy and blessings in each situation. If you are harboring bitterness against anyone (God or man), I urge you to lay it down and begin to find healing in your soul. Look for the hidden blessings. I promise they are there.

As we were completing the edits for this book, Charlie Kirk was assassinated. The world was astonished when, at his memorial, his widow Erica forgave the shooter.[50] Not many of us would be able to forgive such a large offense. But isn't that what Christ asked us to do?[51] After all, how could we ever repay the debt we owe Him?

---

[50] Erika Kirk on Husband's Assassin: "I forgive him." C-Span. Video. YouTube. Retrieved from https://www.youtube.com/watch?v=9OUj_Hzgnjs
[51] Matthew 18:21

REFLECTION:

Read the scriptures listed above, then reflect on them below. Pick out keywords, verses, and themes. Write down how those might apply to your life.

Take a moment and reflect on God's forgiveness. Ask if you have anything in you that needs to be confessed. Embrace that forgiveness. Then, consider anyone else that you need to forgive and forgive them.

_____

_____

_____

_____

_____

_____

_____

_____

_____

_____

_____

_____

_____

DR. KIM MENDOZA

PRAYER:

Lord, forgive anything that is not of you. Help me to accept your grace and make me whole and new. If there are people I need to forgive, help me to forgive them. Amen.

WRITE YOUR OWN PRAYER:

_____

_____

_____

_____

_____

_____

_____

_____

_____

_____

_____

_____

_____

TODAY'S CHALLENGE: This may be the hardest one in this entire book, but I challenge you to call, write, or go see someone you hold a grudge against, and tell him or her that you forgive him or her.

ᨖ **DAY 8** ᨖ

Eliminating the Needles

Those who consider themselves religious and yet do
not keep a tight rein on their tongues deceive
themselves, and their religion is worthless.
(James 1:26, NIV).

"Each person has a tongue and a voice.
These instruments of speech can be used
destructively or employed constructively."
(Rev. Billy Graham, America's Pastor)

DAILY READING:

James 3; Psalm 141:3; Psalm 34:13; Proverbs 21:23;
Ephesians 4:29

DAILY THOUGHT:

Needles cause smoke, not fire. They often smother a
fire. When I think of our mouth, it also has the ability

to smother our fire and just cause smoke—choking out our witness.

Our mouth is like needles. It has the ability to smother our witness. Here are four ways our mouth will get us in trouble:

1. The first one often puts Christians in a bad light—*EXHIBITING FRUSTRATION* AT OTHER PEOPLE. Imagine you're standing in line and the lady behind the counter makes you angry. You grumble. You verbally complain. Then, you tell her off. You feel better and go about your day. But like a stack of dominoes, you may have set something vile in motion. Maybe now she's in a bad mood, and yells at a guest. The boss overhears this and fires her. She goes home and yells at her husband. Her husband now yells at her daughter. The child holds onto that for years and needs therapy to get over it. Okay, maybe that's a bit dramatic. But hopefully, you get the point. Though all interactions are not so stage-worthy, there are times when those dominoes fall. Our one action could have been avoided,

but instead, it can produce a chain effect of negativity. Our words have the power to offer life or death.[52] What if you are the only Christ someone will ever meet? Did you do Him justice with your actions?

2. The second "mouth issue" is when we **GOSSIP or CRITICIZE**. Christians like to say things like, "We need to pray for so and so, because she did this and that," as if prayer permits us to share someone's deepest, darkest secrets. Or if we're upset with them, that somehow warrants us to criticize them. The Bible tells us to stay away from such people.[53] Clearly, God doesn't condone this behavior, and I believe this is why...

I have two sons and two grandsons. I love them to death. So, no one better talk bad about them. If you have kids (or even nieces, nephews, or siblings), you probably feel the same way. So,

---

[52] Proverbs 18:21
[53] Proverbs 20:19; Leviticus 19:16

here is the kicker… <u>Every</u> human on this planet is God's creation. He molded them. He loves them. He cares about them. Even while we were still sinners, Jesus loved us.[54]

So, when you are gossiping or complaining about someone, you are bad-mouthing one of God's kids (or at the very least, someone He loved enough to die for). Our words have the power to destroy others or bless them.[55]

3. The third way is when we **SPEAK NEGTIVELY ABOUT OURSELVES.** Instead of speaking blessings over ourselves, we speak curses. Psychologists have proven negative words have power.[56] What you speak into existence will likely define your future. You have the power to speak life into your experience. But negative words are defeating.

---

[54] Romans 5:8

[55] Ephesians 4:29

[56] Nevid, J. S. (2024). The psychological power of words. *Psychology Today.*

4. Lastly, we come to the **FOUL MOUTH**. A lot of Christians think it is okay to curse or tell dirty jokes—sometimes boldly without remorse and sometimes in hushed tones (as if one's volume cancels out the power of a curse word). But Christians, please hear me. People are watching. What sets us apart? James 1:26 states that an unbridled tongue equals a *"worthless religion."* Ephesians 5:4 tells us there should not be "<u>any</u> filthiness, foolish talk, or crude joking." If we are cussing or telling dirty jokes, how effective is our witness? How valuable is our walk?[57]

DAILY STORY:

For several years, I owned a small theater called LimeLite. It was a family-friendly venue, which meant no off-color jokes, foul language, or vulgar behavior was allowed. Though a lot of our actors and patrons were Christian, many were not. However, everyone respected the rules, to the point, people would yell out, "That's not LimeLite friendly," even when they

---

[57] James 1:26

were somewhere else. My husband and I made a stand. Honestly, I find it refreshing when someone changes a "word" or apologizes when they forget.

Here's a test. If Jesus were to walk in, would you stop talking or telling a joke? Would you quickly replace a word? If you're a Christian, He is already there. No amount of whispering will hide it. Ask, am I honoring the Lord with my speech or making the Holy Spirit cringe?[58]

---

[58] Ephesians 4:30

REFLECTION:

Read the scriptures listed above, then reflect on them below. Pick out keywords, verses, and themes. Write down how those might apply to your life.

There are 43 verses[59] about the power of words. What do you struggle with? Complaining? Gossip or criticism of others? Cussing? Reflect on whether you build people up or tear them down.

_____

_____

_____

_____

_____

_____

_____

_____

_____

_____

_____

_____

_____

[59] Check it out: https://bible.knowing-jesus.com/topics/The-Power-Of-Words

PRAYER:

Lord, forgive me for things I have said about others. Help me not to curse or criticize. But honor you with my words. Amen.

WRITE YOUR OWN PRAYER:

_____

_____

_____

_____

_____

_____

_____

_____

_____

_____

_____

_____

_____

_____

_____

TODAY'S CHALLENGE: I dare you to not use any cuss words, tell any dirty jokes, gossip, or complain for the next 3 weeks. Can you do it?

PART II
BUILDING A FOUNDATION
"PRAYER & THE WORD"

The next step in building a fire is to create a foundation to protect it. This is usually done with stones. Sometimes the cracks may be filled with clay or other filler to create a solid foundation. As we read in Matthew 7:24-27, a solid foundation is pivotal to our faith. If our faith is built on sand, our spiritual house will crumble. But if it is built on the Rock, it can stand the test of time. In order to continue to build our fiery faith, we need a firm foundation.

"On Christ,
the Solid Rock I stand,
all other ground is sinking
sand."

(Edward Mote, 1834)

ᵂ **DAY 9** ᵂ

Reading the Safety Manual

Your word is a lamp to my feet
and a light to my path.
(Psalm 119:105, NIV)

"A thorough knowledge of the Bible
is worth more than a college education."
(President Theodore Roosevelt)

DAILY READING:

II Timothy 3:14-17; Hebrews 4:12; Joshua 1:8-9;
Romans 15:4

DAILY THOUGHT:

Fire safety is important. Most of us might not read a safety manual before starting a fire, but maybe we should. Can you imagine trying to put together a desk with 100-plus parts from Ikea without any instructions? If you're lucky, it might resemble something, but most likely won't be what you intended. To make things work properly—it all starts with directions from the one who created it.

God didn't leave us to figure everything out on our own. He gave us the Holy Bible. I like how one pastor put it: "Prayer is us talking to God, and the Bible is God talking to us." Our lives become disasters when we construct them on our own, ignoring the Creator's blueprint.

Over the years, many people have told me they don't have time to read the Bible. I ask, "Why do you have time to eat?" They respond, "Well, I have to eat." I ask, "What would happen if you stopped eating?" They say, "I'd get sick or die." I answer, "Exactly. Our spiritual bodies need to be fed, too. Starve them, and they die." A study by Lifeway Research (2019) found that fewer than 32% of Protestants read their Bibles every day, 12% read it once a week, and 12% never read it.[60] The late Reverend Billy Graham once said, "The Bible is not an option; it is a necessity. You cannot grow spiritually strong without it."[61]

---

[60] Earls, A. (2019). How often do you read the Bible. Lifeway Research.
[61] Graham, B. (2021). Why should I read the Bible? Billy Graham Evangelistic Association.

DAILY STORY:

I grew up reading the Bible with my mom at night time before I said my prayer and went to sleep. As I became an adult, I defaulted to that pattern. I read my daily chapter and checked my spiritual duty off. The problem was, I wasn't really digesting anything. The Bible wasn't "meat" for my soul.[62] It was merely a "religious tool." *Religion* is mankind checking a box, but a *relationship* takes quality time.

This forty-day challenge is meant to get people back to reading God's Word and praying. To weed out the distractions and return to the basics of holy living. We need to nourish our souls, which starts by delving into the scriptures. The Bible is the living Word of God—God-breathed.[63] If we want to know what God wants, we start there.

For those of you who struggle, here's a helpful tip. Rather than forcing yourself to read a quota of chapters every night (you may not be digesting it anyway), try writing down a single passage and reflecting on that all day. God prefers *quality* time in our hearts, not quantity of verses just as checklists.[64]

---

[62] I Corinthians 3:2
[63] II Timothy 3:16
[64] Luke 10:38-40

Another idea...you might try reading while you're eating. Then you're feeding both your body and spirit. Whatever works, just devour the Bible daily. The more you read His words, the more you will understand His heart.

REFLECTION:

Read the scriptures listed above, then reflect on them below. Pick out keywords, verses, and themes. Write down how those might apply to your life.

Plan on how you might build the Word of God into your daily lifestyle. Find a verse that you can meditate on today, tomorrow, and the next day.

_____

_____

_____

_____

_____

_____

_____

_____

_____

_____

_____

_____

_____

_____

_____

_____

_____

_____

_____

_____

_____

_____

_____

_____

_____

_____

_____

_____

_____

_____

_____

_____

_____

_____

_____

_____

PRAYER:

Lord, let me be hungry for your word. Help me to understand your message and apply it to my life. Amen.

WRITE YOUR OWN PRAYER:

_____

_____

_____

_____

_____

_____

_____

_____

_____

_____

_____

_____

_____

_____

_____

_____

_____

TODAY'S CHALLENGE: Google seven verses for any area of your life you need to grow in. Then write down those seven scriptures on a sticky. Each day for the next week, carry the "daily" scripture with you. Put it on your mirror where you get ready. Put it on the dashboard of your car. Place it next to your computer screen at work. Stick it on your TV remote. Then reflect on it throughout the day.

🔥 **DAY 10** 🔥

Setting the Tinder

Pray continually.
(I Thessalonians 5:17, NIV).

"Prayer is as natural an expression of faith
as breathing is of life."[65]
(Rev. Jonathan Edwards, 18th Century Preacher)

DAILY READING:
Luke 18:1-8; Romans 8:26-30; James 4:3

DAILY THOUGHT:
Tinder is the initial fuel used to ignite a fire. It is dry and catches fire quickly, making it a great ignition source. If you are experiencing spiritual dryness, pray. Prayer is our ignition source. If we desire a fiery faith, we need to start with daily prayer.

---

[65] Beck, P. (2010). *The voice of faith: Jonathan Edward's theology of prayer.* Sola Scriptura Ministries International.

A pastor friend of mine used to get irritated at red lights. He said he had a bit of "road rage" in his heart. Determined to change, he decided whenever there was a red light, he would pray instead. Red lights became such a positive occurrence that he started to be bummed when the light turned green.

I loved that he turned a frustration into another chance to pray. As I often say, **prayer is not an appointment, it is a lifestyle:** That means we don't mark thirty minutes on our calendar and mark the task "done," but rather, we pray throughout our day. Some of us (I've been guilty before), pray when things are bad or when we need something, but consider any friendship. What if your friend only came to you when they needed something? How long would that friendship last? How intimate could that relationship be? We need to pray constantly and consistently. That means—not stopping, always interceding. Praying without ceasing.[66]

DAILY STORY:

I've attended a few writing conferences, where Jerry Jenkins (co-author of the *Left Behind* series) was the keynote speaker. He shared about interviewing the

---

[66] I Thessalonians 5:17

late (great) Billy Graham. Jerry asked "America's Pastor" how he was so successful.[67] Reverend Graham replied something like, "I never stop praying. Even as I am sitting here with you, I am praying."

What a great example of what we should aspire to do. The more we pray, the more we begin to understand the heart of God. Imagine if we could be so in tune with God that we don't have to pray for His will because we already know it.

---

[67] San Diego Christian Writer's Conference (2006); Write to Publish (2023)

REFLECTION:

Read the scriptures listed above, then reflect on them below. Pick out keywords, verses, and themes. Write down how those might apply to your life.

Continue to pray throughout your day. How can you interweave talking to God into your routine?

_____

_____

_____

_____

_____

_____

_____

_____

_____

_____

_____

_____

_____

_____

_____

Matchbook

PRAYER:

Lord, show me how to pray without ceasing. Give me a hunger to desire to spend time with you. Amen.

WRITE YOUR OWN PRAYER:

_____

_____

_____

_____

_____

_____

_____

_____

_____

_____

_____

_____

_____

_____

_____

_____

TODAY'S CHALLENGE: To get into the habit, set an alarm to go off every hour. Say a prayer. We often have our Fitbits set to tell us when to walk. Our water bottles to tell us when to drink. How often do we think to pray as much?

🔥 DAY 11 🔥
Pitching the Wet Wood

Do not conform to the pattern of this world,
but be transformed by the renewing of your mind.
Then you will be able to test and approve what God's
will is—His good, pleasing and perfect will.
(Romans 12:2, NIV).

"How can you give up the world?
Just do what you ought to do,
and it will give you up."
(Jack Hyles, 20th Century Pastor)

DAILY READING:
Proverbs 3; II Timothy 3:1-9

DAILY THOUGHT:
Though most wood burns, wet wood just smokes. As I mentioned before, smoke can choke out a fire. We need good fuel, so we need to toss out the bad.

In this challenge, one person said, "You're asking a lot." Perhaps I am, but this challenge is no different from the one Jesus posed to His church 2,000 years ago. Jesus asked us to be "set apart." [68] To not "conform" to the world's thinking.[69] This means we are called to live a life that mirrors Christ, not the world. John wrote, "Whoever claims to live in Him must live as Jesus did." [70] Unfortunately, the church is often asleep or invisible. Why would anyone desire to be a Christian when we appear the same as they do? What would be the point? We are to be a light in the darkness.[71] In truth, we cannot please God and be worldly.[72] The Bible states we need to choose a side.[73]

DAILY STORY:

For decades, I found being different from the world challenging. I was a people pleaser. (Do I have any other people pleasers out there?) People pleasers like

---

[68] Deuteronomy 14:2
[69] Romans 12:2
[70] I John 2:6
[71] John 1:5
[72] James 4:4
[73] II Corinthians 6:14

to be liked. Because I was more about pleasing men than God, I held labels like "Casual Christian" or "Closet Christian." In Matthew 10:32-33, Jesus states that He will only acknowledge us before the Father if we do the same for Him. If our lives echo a fallen society, are we acknowledging Christ? I say this, because the title "Christian" means we are to be an imitator of Christ. One night, as I was finishing up the challenge with one church group, two of the women said they were "sad the forty days were over." They feared they would not be able to continue this level of devoutness. My response was that this has to become a *lifestyle*. It's not something we "do," but rather, it's who we are.

So, what happens on day forty-one? This is about walking a path that is honorable to God's purpose for our lives. Consider this book a redirect that will set you up for the rest of your life. If you're already on fire for God, let this time be one of building intimacy and purpose. We have never "arrived" until we are sitting at the feet of Jesus in Heaven. The Bible states we have all fallen short of God's glory.[74] The time for neutrality is over, as being an "authentic" Christian (living by biblical guidance[75]) is no longer popular. However, we should not be surprised. Scripture indicates that the world will hate those who serve Him. [76] That those who live a godly life will be persecuted.[77] Living for Christ is not always easy, but I have found the closer we get to God, the less we want the "worldly stuff." When we give in and give up, our lives are always better.

In these last days, it is not easy to be a Christian, so we must seek first His kingdom[78] and follow His words. I love the quote for today. Do what you're supposed to do (according to God), and the world will *quit you.* If you're trying to please the world, you are not pleasing God. We know this because Jesus said the world would not love us.[79] It's a harsh truth, but accurate. If the world is mad at you, chances are, you're on target.

---

[74] Romans 3:23
[75] James 1:22
[76] II Corinthians 6:14
[77] II Timothy 3:12
[78] Matthew 6:33
[79] John 15:18-19

We have hit a new era where what is good is called bad and what is bad is called good.[80] Moral living has become black and white, and the gray is disappearing, mainly due to the fact, it is no longer popular to be a Christian. We have to step over the line and make a hard decision. Do we want to live for Christ or the world? We have to choose.[81]

---

[80] Isaiah 5:20
[81] Acts 17:30

REFLECTION: Read the scriptures listed above, then reflect on them below. Pick out keywords, verses, and themes. Write down how those might apply to your life.

Write down the things in your life that do not fall in line with "godly living," and plan to get rid of them.

_____

_____

_____

_____

_____

_____

_____

_____

_____

_____

_____

_____

_____

_____

DR. KIM MENDOZA

PRAYER: Lord, help me to give up all the things that keep me from being truly godly. Amen.

WRITE YOUR OWN PRAYER:

_____

_____

_____

_____

_____

_____

_____

_____

_____

_____

_____

_____

_____

_____

_____

_____

_____

DAILY CHALLENGE: The Bible states that if we do not acknowledge Jesus, He will deny us to the Father.[82] If the world loves you, then it may not be clear where you stand. For today's challenge, do something that clearly reveals you are a Christian. Examples: Put a Bible verse on social media. Share Jesus with someone. Bring your Bible to work. Be bold in your faith. Let your light shine before men![83]

---

[82] Matthew 10:33
[83] Matthew 5:16

🔥 **DAY 12** 🔥

Igniting the Toxic Branch

Peace, I leave with you; my peace I give to you.
Not as the world gives do I give to you.
Let not your hearts be troubled,
neither let them be afraid.
(John 14:27, NIV).

"God is above all and beneath all and outside of all
and inside of all. He is above, but not pushed up,
beneath but not depressed, outside, but not
excluded, inside but not confined. He is above all,
presiding, underneath all, sustaining. Outside of all,
embracing, and inside of all, filling.
This is God. He's enough."
(A.W. Tozer, Preacher and Author).

DAILY READING:
II Corinthians 4, 9:8; James 1:17

DAILY THOUGHT:

Imagine that you picked up some kindling. You perceive it to be good for starting a fire. You bring it back to the campfire and toss it in. The entire group freaks out. Why? Come to find out, you just tossed in dried poison ivy.

The wrong perception can be destructive to our spiritual life. Perception has power. Have you ever seen the meme of a pretty girl who looks into a mirror, but sees someone ugly? Or the kitty who sees a lion? One author wrote, "Other people's perception of you is a reflection of them; your response to them is an awareness of you." [84] *Perception.* How we see ourselves and others often has a profound influence on our thinking. How we view God will often dictate our actions. For this reason, it is important to align our perceptions with God's insight, not the worlds.

---

[84] Bennett, R. T. (2021). *The Light in the Heart.* Independently Published.

DAILY STORY:

I will never forget when the Repo Man came. Like many others in 2010, as I mentioned in Day 3, I lost a lot. I didn't truly panic until they carted my minivan away in the middle of the night. I had no idea how I was going to get my kids to school in the morning. I put the word out on an email that I needed a car and prayed for a miracle. Within hours, the phone rang. A friend of mine had an old car for sale for $1,000. With the help of our family, we were able to scrape the money together, and she delivered the car within an hour of when I needed it. The finale—my kids arrived at school on time, and I made it to work. Now, I could have viewed that old "jalopy" of a car as a frustration and been discouraged, but instead, I saw God's beautiful chariot in my driveway. I loved that car! Sure, it wasn't pretty, but it ran well and got me where I needed to go. My perception was one of thankfulness, not irritation. I saw the car for what it was—*a gift from God.*

Our blessing is not always obvious. When we are in a trial, we have to learn to change our perception—to see God's provision, wait for the miracle, and/or watch for a sign. If our focus is on the negative only, we cannot find joy in the journey. Negativity is quite toxic. Years ago, I worked for a company that had some major issues. Daily, people would stand in the hallways and share how upset they were about this or that. Or how hurt a leader made them feel. Or how the processes were stupid and made them do twice as much work. Complain, complain, complain. Always negative, never positive. Reflecting back now, there were positive things... had we all been looking for them. There were great people who worked there. The location was amazing. The product was good. Sure, there were indeed problems, but rather than helping to find solutions or getting on our knees to pray, we chose to spend our days pouring salt water over a Christian company. (That company of 1,000 is now barely alive.) The Bible states that both salt water and fresh water cannot come out of the same mouth.[85] Are you cursing your situation? Do you only see the bad or can you find God's hand? Perception has power. Your focus matters. Ultimately, if you only focus on the negative, then you'll feel the impact of negativity. Also,

---

[85] James 3:11-12

something to consider, you are basically telling God He made a mistake. He made a mistake when He made you look the way you look. He made a mistake when He gave you the spouse you prayed for. He made a mistake when He blessed you with a job.

Now to clarify, I am not trying to say your current situation is rosy or that your trial isn't real. You may be in a very bad situation and desperately need God to get you out. What I am saying is, it is important that if you are complaining and not praying, your problem will get worse. Because instead of finding joy in the midst of the storm, you are focused on the waves. There is no peace in that. Your perception about what is happening can change, if you let it.

Have you ever heard of *Pollyanna*? It was a movie about a young girl who played the "Glad Game," where she found joy in everything. My favorite part of the movie was following a church service. The pastor was a real fire and brimstone pastor, so the congregation hated Sundays. One of the maids asked Pollyanna how she could possibly be "glad" about Sundays. Pollyanna thought for a moment and then replied, "It's a whole week before there's another one."[86]

Next time you face a trial, I encourage you to shift your perception and find God's hidden blessing. Your mindset can be a toxin to your attitude and spiritual life or a gateway to freedom for your soul. You decide.

---

[86] *Pollyanna.* (1960). Walt Disney Productions.

REFLECTION: Read the scriptures listed above, then reflect on them below. Pick out keywords, verses, and themes. Write down how those might apply to your life.

Thank God for all the good things He has done.

_____

_____

_____

_____

_____

_____

_____

_____

_____

_____

_____

_____

_____

_____

_____

_____

_____

_____

_____

_____

_____

_____

_____

_____

_____

_____

_____

_____

_____

_____

_____

_____

_____

_____

_____

_____

_____

PRAYER: Lord, help me to focus on the blessings rather than the trial. Thank you for those times when things seemed bleak, but you protected me. Amen

WRITE YOUR OWN PRAYER:

_____

_____

_____

_____

_____

_____

_____

_____

_____

_____

_____

_____

_____

_____

_____

_____

TODAY'S CHALLENGE: Take something (or someone) you feel negatively about and write down at least three positive observations about that thing (or person). Then, if you haven't listed it already, write down three positive comments about things that apply to you, like your house, your car, your job, your parents, your kids, etc.

🔥 DAY 13 🔥

Striking with Focus

My eyes are ever on the LORD,
for only he will release my feet from the snare.
(Psalm 25:15, NIV).

"Focus on giants, you stumble.
Focus on God, your giants tumble"
(Max Lucado, Author of *Facing your Giants*).

DAILY READING:
Hebrews 12:1-13; Psalm 16

DAILY THOUGHT:

If we're going to light a fire, we need to be attentive to what we are doing. What would happen if we struck the match but weren't looking? We would waste the single, fleeting opportunity for a spark. We would miss the tinder, and the start of the flame—our moment of ignition—would be lost to the wind.

In this scenario, Jesus is the focused target. We need to keep our eyes locked on Him. If we strike out on our own, our energy is misdirected, our focus is lost, and the vital spark of the Holy Spirit, which is meant to ignite our hearts, simply falls into the ash.

Another metaphor I like is the rickety bridge. Have you ever watched a jungle movie where a character is on a rickety rope bridge? Someone yells, "Don't look down!" Of course, the character always looks down and becomes paralyzed by the big chasm and violent current below.

This imagery can reflect our spiritual lives. When we focus on our troubles, our fears, our doubts—we often become paralyzed, unable to take the next step.

The secret to crossing the bridge isn't building a more solid bridge (who has time for that?), but in where we choose to focus. Imagine Jesus is on the other side of the unstable bridge, beckoning us to come across. If we keep our eyes on Him, He will guide us where to step. As Jeremiah wrote, God has a plan, and that plan is not to harm us.[87] If we trust Him, He will help us to the other side of our trial. However, if we look down at

---

[87] Jeremiah 29:11

our circumstances, we too can become paralyzed, back away, or quit.

How do we apply this? We don't look to our left and right. We don't focus on what the bank account says. We don't focus on the naysayers and negative people around us. We don't focus on the problems and trials. We lift our heads and keep our eyes on our Savior. He will direct our path.[88]

Even better than Jesus calling out directions, is Jesus crossing by our side. I like how Moses wrote it: "Be strong and courageous. Do not be afraid or terrified because of them, for the LORD your God goes with you; He will never leave you nor forsake you."[89] Jesus tells us where to step, but He is right next to us the entire way.

DAILY STORY:

Recently, my family had several financial crises back-to-back. Tensions were high, tempers were short, and feelings were hurt. Our focus was on the problem, not on Jesus. And we knew better. This wasn't the first time (nor would it be the last), where we had to solely rely on God's bank account. In our experience, He had

---

[88] Proverbs 3:5-6
[89] Deuteronomy 31:6

always written the check, and it had never bounced once. The next morning, I opened my Two-Year Bible and read the Old Testament scripture for the day. It said, "God stands with the poor and needy."[90] Then, on my way to work that morning, I turned on the radio and a song by J. Moss came on called, "God's Got It." In the song, he sings that he's not worried about the money. Instantly, I reset my thinking. That night, I went to my prayer corner and prayed for peace over the situation, our marriage, and our household. I prayed for provision, wisdom, and direction. But mostly, I prayed for my relationship with Jesus. I asked that I not be tripped up by the stress of finances, but rather, always focus on Him. I placed everything on the altar again, because I knew God has "got it." All of it. We are not alone in our journey. Are we letting Jesus carry our burden? Or are we so focused on our burden that we can't see His empty arms stretched out, ready to carry our load?

Moments like this remind me of a poem from my childhood: "Footprints in the Sand."* In the poem, a character walks along the beach with Jesus, looking back at her life, marked by footprints in the sand. During the darkest moments of her life, there were

---

[90] Psalm 109:22

only one set of footprints. She asks Jesus, "Why would you abandon me in such hard times?" Jesus replies, "It was then that I carried you."[91]

This compelling imagery reminds us that even when we feel utterly alone, we are not. We can be so focused on our struggles that we fail to recognize the presence of a loving God carrying us through the darkest moments. The world is scary, and if that is where your focus is, then you will be afraid. How could you not? But if we keep our eyes on Jesus, let Him direct our lives, and trust Him—there is <u>nothing</u> to fear.[92]

*(For copyright reasons, I'm not putting the entire poem in, but I highly recommend looking it up.)

---

[91] Stevenson, Mary. "Footprints in the Sand." Gold Leaf Press, 1994
[92] Psalm 56:3

REFLECTION: Read the scriptures listed above, then reflect on them below. Pick out keywords, verses, and themes. Write down how those might apply to your life.

Ask, what is under my bridge that distracts me from Jesus? How can I get my eyes back on Jesus?

_____

_____

_____

_____

_____

_____

_____

_____

_____

_____

_____

_____

_____

_____

_____

PRAYER: Lord, help me learn to trust you more. To not be so focused on the problems that I forget to turn to you to help me with them. Amen.

WRITE YOUR OWN PRAYER:

_____

_____

_____

_____

_____

_____

_____

_____

_____

_____

_____

_____

_____

_____

_____

_____

_____

TODAY'S CHALLENGE: I want you to read the following statement, then immediately take inventory of your emotional reaction: The world is scary, as we are dealing with global diseases, fires, earthquakes, flooding, inflation, the threat of World War III, extreme weather, and impending persecution of Christians.

Now, did any of those actually frighten you at any level? If they did, then you're focused on the wrong thing. Is that list scary? Sure. But do we need to worry about any of them? No, if our eyes are on Jesus. God said He would meet all our needs.[93] If we die, then we know we are going to Heaven[94] (and I promise, there you'll be good then). I speak from experience. I lived in anxiety and fear for years, but when I learned to center my attention on Jesus, it was so freeing. I no longer worried about what *could* happen. I had peace, knowing that my Heavenly Father knew what He was doing, and I just needed to rely on Him. Period.

---

[93] Philippians 4:19
[94] II Corinthians 5:8

🔥 DAY 14 🔥

Listening to Smokey

My sheep hear my voice,
and I know them, and they follow me.
(John 10:27, NIV).

"We often miss hearing God's voice simply
because we aren't paying attention"
(Rick Warren, Author of the *Purpose Driven Life*).

DAILY READING:

I Samuel 3; John 8:47; Jeremiah 33:3; Exodus 20:8-9

DAILY THOUGHT:

Anyone who camped a lot as a kid, may remember Smokey Bear. The name originally came from a bear cub who was rescued from a wildfire. He became the "spokesperson" for the U.S. Forest Service to remind people about fire safety.[95] One famous ad has Smokey Bear tipping his hat saying, "Thanks for Listening."[96] If people ignore the rules for fire safety, it may become a dangerous problem, especially from California to New Mexico where vegetation is dry.

Ignoring God's voice can also be dangerous. Sometimes we can be so busy, we can't hear Him. Did you know there is a whistle that only kids and dogs can hear? It is inaudible to people over the age of thirty. After a certain age, our ears are no longer attuned to that frequency. This illustration is symbolic of how we hear God. When the noise of life surrounds us, we too can lose the ability to hear the frequency of God's voice.

The Holy Spirit requires time to speak into our lives. That might mean turning off social media, YouTube, sports, the computer, or the phone—and spending time in His presence, just listening.

---

[95] Smithsonian Institute Archives. (n.d.) Smokey bear.
[96] Ibid

How many times have we fallen asleep while praying? I imagine God saying, "Wait, I had more to tell you!" Or we share all our requests, then flip on the TV. And God says, "Wait, I wanted to respond." Or we are too busy to pray, and He walks behind us saying, "I really wanted to tell you something, if you'd just stop for a moment and listen." How often do we forget prayer is a two-way conversation? It's possible we don't know God's will because we don't give Him space to share it. Our Heavenly Father has plenty to tell us, but we must be still and listen.

Also, remember that God is not the only one trying to communicate with us. We're told to be sober-minded and watchful, because the enemy prowls around looking for someone to devour.[97] Who is speaking into your life?

Adam and Eve are prime examples of what happens when we let the wrong voice influence us. The first

---

[97] I Peter 5:8

couple on earth allowed the serpent to deceive them, ignoring God, and the rest is history.[98]

It is necessary that we tune out all voices but our Savior's. Our work should never be so consuming, we neglect our time with God. Which brings me to the next point: All of us require a Sabbath*.[99] This day of rest was never a suggestion (though many Christians treat it that way). This command was written by the hand of God, because He knew our bodies, minds, and spirits would benefit from a day off. You might say, it's impossible; I have to work. And I would respond... nothing is impossible when you serve God.[100]

DAILY STORY:

Years ago, I was teaching a college Sunday school class. During prayer time, one young woman shared that particular class would be her last one, because she got a new job. Apparently, the company wanted her to work seven days a week, sixty-plus hours. I challenged her to turn the position down and pray for

---

[98] Genesis 3:1-5
[99] Exodus 20:8
[100] Luke 1:37

a better job. She cringed (as I'm sure most would), but she stepped out in faith and turned it down. Within a few days, she called me excited. "You won't believe it! I just got a nine-to-five, Monday-Friday job that not only has a better schedule but pays more." I did believe it, because I knew God honored her obedience. It is important to realize God's plan for our lives will never go contrary to what He has said before.[101] He will never give us anything that would harm our relationship with Him. (It is important to note that not *every* opportunity is from the Lord. By finding time to be with Him, we can discern His voice—and know.)

Side note: A Sabbath does not have to be on a Saturday or Sunday. If you absolutely need to work on those days, please schedule a sabbath after you've worked six days, per God's design. [102]

---

[101] Hebrews 13:8
[102] Exodus 20:8-9

REFLECTION: Read the scriptures listed above, then reflect on them below. Pick out keywords, verses, and themes. Write down how those might apply to your life.

Think about what God might be trying to tell you today. Are you listening?

_____

_____

_____

_____

_____

_____

_____

_____

_____

_____

_____

_____

_____

_____

_____

PRAYER: Lord, help me to know your voice. Help me to be able to discern when it is the path you would have me travel and when it is me or someone else's will. Amen.

WRITE YOUR OWN PRAYER:

_____

_____

_____

_____

_____

_____

_____

_____

_____

_____

_____

_____

_____

DAILY CHALLENGE: Spend some time just in God's presence—no praying—just listening.

🔥 **DAY 15** 🔥

Sitting around the Ring

For as in one body, we have many members,
and the members do not all have the same function
so, we, though many, are one body in Christ,
and individually members one of another.
(Romans 12:4-5, NIV)

"There has never been a spiritual
awakening in any country or locality
that did not begin in united prayer."
(A.T. Pierson, 19th Century Theologian)

DAILY READING:

I Corinthians 12:12-30; Acts 2:42-47

DAILY THOUGHT:

I have always loved a campfire. It provides us light and warmth as we share stories and roast marshmallows. Unless you're just trying to survive, a campfire is not typically an isolated activity. It is something we share with other people. We were never meant to live in isolation, but rather to dwell in community. [103]

Even in nature, we see the importance of community. Consider the ants. Ant colonies are so bonded they can pass knowledge between generations, survive floods by clumping together, and work quickly and efficiently to complete a project.[104] This bond of ants demonstrates the power of a strong community.

Jesus Himself understood connection. He went to synagogue[105] and had disciples, with whom He shared meals and lived life. The early church actually shared possessions, met together, and supported one another.[106] Christianity is not supposed to be a solo affair. We are the "body" of Christ. Just like the physical body requires bones, a heart, and a brain to function, it is essential to the church body to have various parts.[107] We need disciplined members who

---

[103] Genesis 2:18
[104] National Geographic Society. (n.d.). *Ants. National Geographic.*
[105] Luke 4:16
[106] Acts 2:42-45
[107] I Corinthians 12:12-27

move us. Positive people who inspire us. Wise leaders who direct us. Ecclesiastes says that two are better than one. [108] Paul tells us to bear one another's burdens.[109] Jesus said, when two or more are gathered in His name He is among them.[110]

Community provides accountability. When we pray, we become stronger against wicked forces. No one would go into war alone. In the face of the rising global darkness, we require unwavering unity to fight the spiritual battles we are facing daily.

In addition, the body offers support during trials. Peter's time in prison is a great example of this. The church body *prayed together*, and Peter was able to escape.[111] We need each other now more than ever. Revival may start in one heart, but it never stays there. Great movements of God always happen when a community of people pray together in unity.

---

[108] Ecclesiastes 4:9
[109] Galatians 6:2
[110] Matthew 18:20
[111] Acts 12

DAILY STORY:

Where I grew up, we had annual wildfires. One year in particular, a fire burned on three sides of the city. At the time, I worked at a Christian college, which was housed on the property of a megachurch, along with a Christian high school, and an elementary school. A ribbon of fire cut through the shade of night, eating its way through the dry brush, burning straight for the property of these buildings. Instead of retreating (as any "sane" person might), the pastors of the megachurch stayed in parking lot and prayed. Suddenly, a rush of Wind (worthy of any biblical story), picked up and blew the fire away—all the properties were saved.

When we come together, agree together, pray together, believe together—miracles do happen.

REFLECTION: Read the scriptures listed above, then reflect on them below. Pick out keywords, verses, and themes. Write down how those might apply to your life.

Consider the body of Christ and your function within it. Are you working in your purpose? What is holding you back? Are you keeping anyone else from working in his or her purpose? What might you do to help others walk in their purpose?

_____

_____

_____

_____

_____

_____

_____

_____

_____

_____

_____

_____

PRAYER: Lord, help me have the courage to do what you are calling me to do. May I not do anything in vanity or pride but do all for your glory. Also, enable me to help others reach their full God-given potential. Amen.

WRITE YOUR OWN PRAYER:

_____

_____

_____

_____

_____

_____

_____

_____

_____

_____

_____

_____

_____

_____

TODAY'S CHALLENGE: See if you can find a prayer partner and set up a time to meet and pray for your families, church, community, and country.

🔥 DAY 16 🔥

Nursing the Ember

This is the confidence we have in approaching God:
that if we ask anything according to His will, He hears
us. And if we know that He hears us—whatever we
ask—we know that we have what we asked of Him
(I John 5:14-15, NIV).

"Prayer is the acid test of the inner man's strength. A
strong spirit is capable of praying much and praying
with all perseverance until the answer comes.
A weak one grows weary and fainthearted in the
maintenance of praying."
(Watchman Nee, Author of the *Spiritual Man*)

DAILY READING:

Acts 3:1-10; Mark 5:34; Luke 17:19; Luke 18:42

DAILY THOUGHT:

An ember is not yet a flame, but if we keep nursing it, eventually it will burn bright. Faith starts like an ember, the more we nurse both, the more ignited we become. That is why this book was written. To help people get beyond the spiritual walk of an ember to a roaring fire that rages and starts embers for others.

As I mentioned yesterday, faith matters. God is not so concerned with the outcome as much as He is with our heart in the journey. When we pray, we have to get away from "hoping" God will heal or help us and start believing He will. I think we miss out on miracles simply because we do not *truly* believe the words we are praying. Our mouth says one thing, while our heart has doubts. Scripture says if we have faith the size of a mustard seed (the tiniest seed that grows into one of the largest flowers), we can move mountains.[112] Do we walk in that kind of faith?

I believe that God desires to show us miracles in our lives. He cares about our hurts and the pain of others.

---

[112] Matthew 17:20

Since I began to incorporate true faith into my life, I have witnessed healing and restoration multiple times. Bona fide miracles. A woman healed from cancer. Another woman with chronic kidney stones. Another's back stopped hurting. A child was healed in the womb.

Now, I must make a caveat here. Healing and help may not happen like we think they will. Not all healing is physical, and not all help is determined by *our* desires. I will never advocate for "name it and claim it, prosperity gospel," Christianity, as that is *me*-centric, not *God*-centric. However, I do believe that every prayer receives a response from God. Sometimes it is "Yes." Sometimes it is "No." And sometimes it is "Wait." But He always answers, and His response will be for our benefit. So, we must walk in faith and trust the One who controls the future and directs our lives. He will make the right events happen in *His* timing— but it starts with faith. If you look at the stories about Jesus, there were people who never received their miracle because of their unbelief in Him.[113]

---

[113] Matt. 13:58; 17:19-20

DAILY STORY:

A few years ago, I had a growth in my neck. The doctors feared cancer. I was concerned about the fact that I am a speaker and professor by trade, so I use my throat daily. In faith, I reached out to several pastors to come pray for me. When I returned to the doctor's, it wasn't cancerous, and the growth was gone. About a month after this, I visited a church on a whim. The pastor's wife (one of the ones who had prayed for me) asked if I'd pray for another woman who had a tumor in her throat. I did, and the woman visited the doctor on Monday and had the same ending—she was healed. Praise Jesus! It was by faith[114] that God would heal both of us.

Now, faith does not always come easily to everyone. In fact, how I received mine was strange, but hey, God used a donkey,[115] a burning bush,[116] a fleece,[117] and broken pottery[118] to make His point before. So, with this in mind, I'll admit my faith journey started with a

---

[114] James 5:15
[115] Numbers 22:21-39
[116] Exodus 3:2-4
[117] Judges 6:36-40
[118] Isaiah 30:14

cat. Yes, a cat. I know it's bizarre but go with me. (I promise, I am not a crazy cat lady—yet.)

A few years back, I adopted a rescue kitten who had feline immunodeficiency virus (FIV) which is like AIDS for a cat.[119] This condition is <u>not curable</u>. Since my cat was already symptomatic, the vet said that she would likely die within the year. FIV is a horrible condition. My kitten (Skittles) was covered from head to feet in sores. Her paws were painfully cracked, and she constantly ran a high fever. Just to feel better, the vet gave her a steroid shot every three weeks ($100 a pop). One night, while I was doing my devotion time, Skittles crawled into my lap. She was hot to the touch and covered in lesions. It was clear, she was miserable. With overwhelming compassion, I touched her fur and prayed, "God, would you please heal my cat?" Now, I'll be honest. I had never prayed for an animal, but God did it. He healed her. She has not had a sore, a fever, or any sign of the disease since. Her paws look beautiful. And, at the time of writing this book, she has

---

[119] Editorial WebMD Contributor. (November 2025). "Cats and FIV." WebMD. https://www.webmd.com/pets/cats/cat-fiv-feline-immunodeficiency-virus

been with us for five years. What I learned was, "If God can heal a cat, God can heal…[insert any need here]."

Because I could not deny what happened, my faith grew stronger than ever. Remember, God said if He will take care of the birds surely, He will take care of us.[120] So, I am saying to you, dear reader, if God can heal my cat, He can help or heal you, your parent, your sibling, or your friend—But it starts with faith.[121]

---

[120] Matthew 6:26-34
[121] Romans 1:17

REFLECTION: Read the scriptures listed above, then reflect on them below. Pick out keywords, verses, and themes. Write down how those might apply to your life.

Think about your needs. How is your faith? Do you truly believe that God will answer your prayer?

_____

_____

_____

_____

_____

_____

_____

_____

_____

_____

_____

_____

_____

_____

_____

_____

_____

_____

_____

_____

_____

_____

_____

_____

_____

_____

_____

_____

_____

_____

_____

_____

_____

_____

_____

_____

_____

PRAYER: Lord, help me grow my faith and trust you with the answer. Amen.

WRITE YOUR OWN PRAYER:

_____

_____

_____

_____

_____

_____

_____

_____

_____

_____

_____

_____

_____

_____

_____

_____

TODAY'S CHALLENGE: Consider your doubt. Talk directly about that doubt with Jesus. Confront it. As you pray this week, really pray from the heart.

PART III

ADDING THE FUEL

"TRUST & FAITH"

Fire lives on three things: *heat, fuel,* and *oxygen.* If you snuff any of these out, the flames will disappear. In faith, our *oxygen* is the Holy Spirit who breathes life into us. The *heat* is our faith that fans the flames, and the *fuel* added is building our lives on God's principles (scripture, prayer, and opportunity). Are you ready to fan the flames?
To fully trust God and walk in faith?

"Destitute of the Fire of God,
nothing else counts,
possessing Fire,
nothing else matters"

(Reverend Samuel Chadwick, 1932).

🔥 **DAY 17** 🔥

Watching for Smoke

Keep watch over yourselves and
all the flock of which the Holy Spirit
has made you overseers.
Be shepherds of the church of God,
which he bought with his own blood.
(Acts 20:28, NIV)

"We do not want a church that will move with the
world; we want a church that will move the world."
(G.K. Chesterton, Christian Author & Philosopher)

DAILY READING:
Revelation 3; I John 2

DAILY THOUGHT:
Have you ever tossed a box in the fire, only to find out
there was Styrofoam or plastic coating? Instantly, there
is a plume that stings the eyes and has an unpleasant
odor. This is called "pungent smoke." This smoke

occurs when a fire is smoldered by insufficient oxygen or toxic materials (e.g. plastics). These toxic gases are dangerous and can cause physical damage to one's organs. Using that analogy, let's consider our walk with God. If our Christian walk is just "smoking," and not "on fire," the Bible states that one aroma is pleasant to God and leads to life and the other leads to death. [122] A "smoking" walk is nothing more than lukewarm. The Lord is not happy with a "lukewarm" Christian.

The Scripture reading for this week is challenging. It examines how well the early churches were (or weren't) doing. The author John harshly criticizes the *lukewarm* church in Laodicea (modern Turkey).[123] Laodicea was a wealthy city, located near major trade routes. The assumption is that most of the Christians in this church worked in trade, i.e., buying and selling. In addition, the culture of Laodicea worshiped the emperor, so the Christians began to be persecuted in the area. This started to affect their sales and hurt their bottom line. The Laodicean Christians were so focused on their

---

[122] II Corinthians 2:15-16; Isaiah 3:24
[123] Revelation 3:14-22

financial loss and the pleasures of the world, they developed spiritual apathy.[124]

DAILY STORY:

As mentioned above, tepid faith puts a bad taste in God's mouth. Consider lukewarm coffee. I am a huge coffee snob. My friends and family know I love coffee, but not just *any* coffee. It has to be what I consider "good coffee." I will drive forty-five minutes away just to get my favorite brand. I love coffee. Coffee is a blanket to my insides, and every morning, I savor that first sip. However, I don't always take the last sip. Why? Because for me, lukewarm coffee tastes horrible; its purpose ("a blanket to my insides") is gone.

Likewise, lukewarm water has little use on its own, however, if you boil water on a hot stove, the liquid begins to move, it has purpose, and can produce more (e.g., pasta, steep tea, or best of all, brew coffee). Our faith is no different. If we are lukewarm, we are stagnant and a disappointment to God. We lack our God-designed purpose. It is only when we turn up the heat in our walks that things start moving and we are able to achieve mighty things for the Kingdom of God.

---

[124] Sauter, M. (2025). The church of Laodicea in the Bible and archaeology. Biblical Archaeology Society.

This entire challenge is about igniting (or fanning) the fire in your spiritual walk so you can do remarkable things for Jesus. Stay focused, do the work, and you will be a sweet aroma unto the Lord.[125]

---

[125] II Corinthians 2:15-16

REFLECTION: Read the scriptures listed above, then reflect on them below. Pick out keywords, verses, and themes. Write down how those might apply to your life.

Think about your own walk and the concept of apathetic Christianity. How much of the world takes your focus? How hot is your faith?

_____

_____

_____

_____

_____

_____

_____

_____

_____

_____

_____

_____

_____

_____

_____

_____

_____
_____
_____
_____
_____
_____
_____
_____
_____
_____
_____
_____
_____
_____
_____
_____
_____
_____
_____
_____
_____

PRAYER: Lord, please show me any part of myself that is lukewarm. Help me to be strength to complete this journey and be on fire for you. Amen.

WRITE YOUR OWN PRAYER:

_____

_____

_____

_____

_____

_____

_____

_____

_____

_____

_____

_____

_____

_____

_____

_____

TODAY'S CHALLENGE: As if you were Paul, write a letter to yourself. What are you doing well? What do you need to work on? How can you do your part in the body of Christ?

🔥 DAY 18 🔥

Obtaining the Fuel

And my God will meet all your needs according
to the riches of his glory in Christ Jesus.
(Philippians 4:19, NIV)

"Where God guides, God provides"
(Ancient Proverb, Original Author Unknown).

DAILY READING: *I Kings 17; Mark 6:35-44;*
Deuteronomy 28:1-14

DAILY THOUGHT:

How often do we worry about bills or the lack of
resources? Day in and day out, we center our thoughts
on what we don't have. But there are several promises
in God's Word that demonstrate He cares about us

and our needs.[126] He will provide. Can you fully trust God with all that your require?

DAILY STORY:

A while back, I was struggling with a lack of faith. I had some problems, and though I prayed, I wasn't confident He had me. Then one weekend, I went camping with my son. Friday, we arrived at the campground after sunset and couldn't find our reserved spot in the dark. We stopped looking and prayed. By the time we said "amen," some random guy showed up and told us the location. (It was off the road, way up on a hillside. I'm pretty sure we wouldn't have found it without his help.)

Saturday evening, we realized we didn't have enough firewood to make it past 7:00 PM. As we discussed it, a branch fell, furnishing us with enough fuel for the rest of the night.

Sunday morning, before heading back, we decided to go hiking. But we didn't get far, because my pants kept

---

[126] Psalms 23:1; II Corinthians 9:8; Matthew 6:31-32; 7:11; I Peter 5:7

slipping down. I said, "I wish I had a rope or bungee cord to use as a belt." Just then, I happened to glance up in the tree, and a bungee cord hung down.

In that moment, I recognized God's provision. Monday morning, I cut that cord into a bracelet, so whenever I go through tough times, I can wear it as a reminder that if God cares enough to help me with my pants, He cares about everything in my life.

Some might find that story a little silly, but many times in scripture, God used unorthodox ways to make His point. A fish to pay taxes[127], manna from heaven,[128] water from a rock,[129] ravens for food,[130] and oil and flour that don't run out.[131] That weekend, I needed to learn to trust God, and so He provided.

Interestingly enough, as I plugged in the Bible verses (see footnote), I was amazed to see that the number seventeen (17) kept showing up. So, I have gift for you.

---

[127] Matthew 17:24-27
[128] Exodus 16:3-17
[129] Exodus 17:1-6
[130] I Kings 17:4-6
[131] I Kings 17:13-16

Like my bracelet, consider the number "17" as a reminder of provision. On those days you need encouragement, write "17" on a sticky note and place it by your bills, on your mirror, in your wallet, as a reminder—God will provide.

One more illustration for today. Years ago, a therapist said, "Imagine there's a huge 'money monster' at the bottom of a dark and ominous pit, who is attached to a rope. You are holding the other end of the rope. Regularly, the money monster yanks, drawing you closer to the edge. You dig in your heels in, terrified of falling into the pit, but the more you tug, the harder the monster yanks back. Though you're paralyzed in fear, you just need to let go of the rope."

A simple solution—Let. Go. It starts with release. If you struggle with worry, I challenge you to drop "the rope." Furthermore, thank Jesus for the provision you have and what is coming. Trust Him—He has you.

REFLECTION: Read the scriptures listed above, then reflect on them below. Pick out keywords, verses, and themes. Write down how those might apply to your life.

What issue do you need to trust God with? Name your rope.

_____

_____

_____

_____

_____

_____

_____

_____

_____

_____

_____

_____

_____

_____

_____

_____
_____
_____
_____
_____
_____
_____
_____
_____
_____
_____
_____
_____
_____
_____
_____
_____
_____
_____
_____
_____

PRAYER: Dear Lord, give me the faith to trust you will provide. Bless the money that I give to you and bless my family. Amen.

WRITE YOUR OWN PRAYER:

_____

_____

_____

_____

_____

_____

_____

_____

_____

_____

_____

_____

_____

_____

_____

_____

TODAY'S CHALLENGE: Consider all the moments when you know God showed up. Write those down and share one with others.

🔥 **DAY 19** 🔥

Anticipating the Spark

Very truly I tell you,
whoever believes in me will do the works
I have been doing, and they will do even greater
things than these, because I am going to the Father.
(John 14:12, NIV)

"Never be afraid to trust an
unknown future to a known God"
(Corrie ten Boom, author of *The Hiding Place*).

DAILY READING:

Mark 8:22-26; John 9:1-7

DAILY THOUGHT:

Right before the flame, there is a spark. Until that second, we lean in, we anticipate, we prepare another match. But we know the spark will happen, if we just keep trying. Like praying for a miracle, we need to anticipate the flame.

Today's reading is about two people, with the same affliction, who were healed in two different ways. One had an instant healing of blindness, the other one Jesus touched twice. We know from examples in Scripture, Jesus didn't need to "touch" either man to heal them.[132] The man who saw "blurry trees walking around"[133] could have been instantly healed. So, why did Jesus go through the motions? My personal belief, Jesus demonstrated that some miracles take time. That every miracle looks different. What worked for one person, may not be best for another. Like we discussed yesterday, it's about trusting God.

DAILY STORY:

My son was born blind in one eye. There was this website where a person could plug in a birthday, and it would spit out that person's "life verse." When I plugged in my son's birthday, it listed the reference for

---

[132] Matt. 8:5-17; Matt. 9:6-7; Luke 17:14
[133] Mark 8:24

the blurry healing. As his mom, I was elated. I believed he would be healed. I lived on that promise for years, believing he would be healed before he had to take the eye exam for a driver's license. When the day finally came, he still had his affliction. I remember saying, "Okay, Lord, if you're going to do this miracle, you need to do it now." But since it didn't happen (as embarrassing as it is to admit), I told my son, "If you keep your other eye open behind your hand, I think you can still see the letters." And my teenage son responded, "Where is the faith in that?" *Ouch!*

He stepped forward and sure enough, he failed the eye exam. But—there was a second exam given to people who failed the first one. The lady explained, "You can only miss three." Apparently, if he missed four, he wouldn't drive <u>ever</u>.

They made me return to the waiting area. I sat in a hard metal chair and prayed like madwoman. My son stepped up to the machine—missed one. *Pray. Pray. Pray.* Missed two. *Pray. Pray. Pray.* Missed three. The moment of truth... and... exhale... he didn't miss anymore. He passed. He could drive.

Was this miracle the one I wanted? No. But was it adequate for what my son needed? Definitely. My sixteen-year-old son schooled me on faith that day. He reminded me that sometimes the miracle is clear and instant, but sometimes it's fuzzy and takes time. Often, it is completely different from we expect, but God is punctual to meet our needs. If you were to ask my son, he would tell you, "I believe healing will be at the right time, for the right reason and most likely to help someone find Jesus." But he also says, if he is never healed, he's okay with that, because God still sustains him right where he's at. Isn't our God good!

REFLECTION: Read the scriptures listed above, then reflect on them below. Pick out keywords, verses, and themes. Write down how those might apply to your life.

Think of a time when God worked a different miracle than the one you were expecting. Why do you think He chose that path instead? Do you ever have to ask yourself, "Where's the faith in that?"

_____

_____

_____

_____

_____

_____

_____

_____

_____

_____

_____

_____

_____

PRAYER: Lord, help me to trust your plan, even when things do not make sense. Help me use those things in me that may seem like flaws to others but may make me stronger in my faith. Amen.

WRITE YOUR OWN PRAYER:

_____

_____

_____

_____

_____

_____

_____

_____

_____

_____

_____

_____

_____

_____

_____

_____

TODAY'S CHALLENGE: What are you praying for? What would happen if God didn't answer the way you wanted Him to? Dig into that idea. If we can learn to be "okay" with whatever the outcome, we are able to lean into to God more.

♨ DAY 20 ♨

Awaiting the Blaze

But they who wait for the Lord
shall renew their strength.
they shall mount up with wings like eagles.
they shall run and not be weary;
they shall walk and not faint.
(Isaiah 40:31, NIV)

"He didn't make a mistake when he made you a
promise. It was deliberate and intentional.
He knows what he's doing
when he allows you to wait"
(Shanté Grosset, MBS, Vlog Host).

DAILY READING:

Ecclesiastes 3; Proverbs 3:5-6; Psalm 27:14

DAILY THOUGHT:

When it's cold and getting dark, waiting on the fire to flourish is not always easy, but just like our lesson yesterday, sometimes it just takes time. Have you ever heard the expression, *timing is everything*?

In Daniel, we see God promised the Israelites they would go back to their land, but it hadn't happened yet.[134] In the chapter, the angel tells Daniel that he was off to fight a spiritual war regarding the Israelites still being exiled. The fight was on for the promise. Sometimes, spiritual darkness is at work to keep us away from our God-given purpose. Not all roadblocks are physical; sometimes they are spiritual. However, God knows when the timing is right. When everything is perfect according to his will, He will let it happen.

Consider a pregnant woman for a moment. Pregnancy is one of the most uncomfortable experiences a female can go through. She can't wait for the baby to appear. She counts down the days as she prepares the nursery, packs her "go-bag," and starts her maternity leave. All

---

[134] Daniel 10:20-21

she thinks about is holding her sweet infant in her arms. But no matter how much the mother desires this, she would never try to deliver her baby before he or she is fully developed. The longer the baby "cooks" in the womb, the healthier the newborn will be.

Now consider our dreams and desires. While they are "cooking," we should be growing. We shouldn't want them to occur before *we* are fully developed, and the *situation* is right for us. If we push too hard too soon (trying to do it ourselves), either we or the situation may not be complete. Maybe the ministry, career, or opportunity could have been successful, but now it won't be, because we or it was not ready.

DAILY STORY:

The Lord told me I would be a full-time professor. So, for two years, I prayed for my dream job. I filled out a resume a day (that's over 700 resumes for those who are counting), and yet, no one called me for an interview. I was confused and discouraged, but there was more at play than I realized. I later found out a barren woman three states away prayed for a baby. In order for my dream to come true, her prayer had to be answered, too. Once she got her dream, she stepped down, and the position was open for me to fill. This is why we trust God with the timing. He sees all the pieces on the board. In due time, everything will align and make sense. So, if He is ready for you to go somewhere, He will make a way. Let us pray for His will. Pray for His timing. Pray for any spiritual forces that may be standing in the way. And above all, grow while we're waiting.

REFLECTION: Read the scriptures listed above, then reflect on them below. Pick out keywords, verses, and themes. Write down how those might apply to your life.

Define what you're waiting for. What are you worried about? Then write down what it will take to surrender that worry to God.

_____

_____

_____

_____

_____

_____

_____

_____

_____

_____

_____

_____

_____

_____

DR. KIM MENDOZA

PRAYER: Lord, help me release [insert your desire] to you. Help me to trust you and wait on you while you oversee the future. Amen.

WRITE YOUR OWN PRAYER:

_____

_____

_____

_____

_____

_____

_____

_____

_____

_____

_____

_____

_____

_____

_____

_____

_____

TODAY'S CHALLENGE: If you are hard at work to make something happen, stop trying that thing until the challenge is over. It will still be there, but maybe you'll have more clarity and direction.

◢◣ DAY 21 ◢◣

Flourishing in the Gust

He stilled the storm to a whisper;
the waves of the sea were hushed.
(Psalm 107:29, NIV)

"When you come out of the storm,
you won't be the same person who walked in.
That's what this storm is all about."
(Haruki Murakami, Author)

DAILY READING:

Mark 4:3-41; Isaiah 26; Genesis 1

DAILY THOUGHT:

Sometimes when we are trying to ignite a fire, a gust of wind threatens to blow it out. But if we protect it, keep feeding it, and don't give up... it can flourish.

The same is true of our spiritual walks. The Bible doesn't say *if* we will go through trials, but *when* we do go through them. All of us walk through hard times. It is the result of a fallen and broken world. But there are two outcomes to every trial: some grow us, and some destroy us. We determine the outcome. Finding the strength to overcome the trial is not something we are supposed to do alone. We should lean on the Lord.

Let's examine our scripture for today. Jesus is asleep in the boat during a violent storm.[135] Has that ever happened to you? Where it feels like Jesus is taking a nap? Interesting enough, there were at least ten (10) miracles between Matthew 1 and Matthew 8, where we see this story—one of them healing a leaper. You would think their "faith meter" would be maxed out. But instead, they shook Jesus awake, fearful of what might happen to them. And to make it worse, they accused Jesus of not caring.

The fact that Jesus was asleep should have been the first sign that they had nothing to worry about. But

---

[135] Matthew 8:23-27

we'll get back to that. First, Jesus demands the waves and wind to calm down. Why is He able to do this? Because Jesus verbally created the wind and waves (see Genesis); therefore, they knew His voice.[136] He spoke the entire earth into existence, so, this world is subject to its Creator. Nothing that we go through is beyond God's intervention. Therefore, if Jesus is asleep, we have nothing to fear. Imagine for a moment how this story might have changed if the disciples approached Jesus calmly and said, "Hey, Jesus, the storm is a little rough. Would you mind calming it down for us?"

Jesus desires that brand of faith. Over and over, He said the people's *faith* made them whole.[137] Next time you are in the storm of life, simply ask God, "Hey, Jesus, would you mind fixing this for me?" rather than panicking. Or... pray for peace. You are not alone in the storm. He's in the boat. He's got you. You just need to ask for help to get through it.

---

[136] Genesis 1
[137] Matt. 9:22; 28-29; Luke 18:42

DAILY STORY:

Did you ever hear the story about Antoinette Tuff? In 2013, a 20-year-old gunman came into the Discovery Learning Academy in Decatur, Georgia, with an AK-47 assault rifle and 500 rounds of ammunition. There were 800 students and 100 employees present. [138] Antoinette had just lost her husband to another woman; she had received a call that she needed to pay $15,000 or lose her car, and now there was a gunman in her school. Inside she screamed, "God help me." In that moment, she felt the Holy Spirit tell her to love the gunman. She prayed for godly wisdom, and He gave it to her in spades. Following God's lead, she spoke. At one point, he fired a bullet at her face, and it ricocheted. But Tuff stayed in silent prayer and said words like, "It's gonna be all right sweetheart. I just want you to know that I love you, though, okay?" Eventually, the gunman surrendered, and Antoinette saved over 900 people. Why? Because she let the Holy Spirit guide her actions rather than panic. Though she was enduring more than one trial, she remembered who gave her strength.

---

[138] Staff. How one woman's faith stopped a school shooting. Tell Me More.

Trials strengthen us. They prepare us. They make us better. Consider an egg. Before it is boiled, it is easily cracked. But once it has been through the fire, it is solid. Additionally, trials can help us discover what *not* to do in the future. I think of my cat being curious about the toilet. One day, she climbed on top of the seat and fell in. Getting wet was enough to keep her from ever doing that again.

Hopefully, we learn from our trial. If we don't, we may need to go through it again and again. I don't know about you... but once is enough for me. So, I encourage you to persevere, grow, and testify on the other side of your storm.

REFLECTION: Read the scriptures listed above, then reflect on them below. Pick out keywords, verses, and themes. Write down how those might apply to your life.

Write down a time when you were in pain, then reflect on what might have been God's purpose for allowing you to go through that situation.

_____

_____

_____

_____

_____

_____

_____

_____

_____

_____

_____

_____

_____

_____

Matchbook

PRAYER: Lord, I pray you help me walk through the trials of life with a joyful heart. Please show me your purpose in the struggle and give me the strength to endure it and allow me to use the experience for your glory. Amen.

WRITE YOUR OWN PRAYER:

_____

_____

_____

_____

_____

_____

_____

_____

_____

_____

_____

_____

_____

_____

TODAY'S CHALLENGE: Are you panicking? My challenge for you today is to approach Jesus calmly with these words: "Lord, _____ is a little rough, can you calm the storm, either in me, or all together." And then take a nap yourself, knowing God has it.

ᴥ DAY 22 ᴥ
Selecting the Right Log

Many are the plans in the mind of a man,
but it is the purpose of the LORD that will stand.
(Proverbs 19:21, NIV)

"A wiling heart is the first step
in finding God's will in our lives.
We cannot expect God to force us
or to plead with us about the calling in our lives"
(Dr. David Jeremiah, Author & Pastor).

DAILY READING:

*Matthew 6:33; I Thessalonians 5:18; James 1:5;
Proverbs 3:5-6*

DAILY THOUGHT:

Knowing what to do when your fire threatens to go out is not always easy. Often, the right fuel can be the perfect antidote to our fire gaining intensity. But how do we know which is the correct log? If the "burn master" is still with us, we can ask Him.

How often have you prayed for the Lord's will? There are thousands of books on the subject. Preachers (including myself) love to preach on how to discover God's perfect plan for one's life. Most Christians search endlessly for that single nugget that explains their spiritual (and physical) destiny. The problem is discovering the Lord's plan won't come from a quick conversation, a self-help book, or a sermon. *Knowing* His true will for your life takes time in the Holy Spirit's presence.

Consider this. Over time, a mother knows when something is wrong or when her baby wants something. Studies have shown a mother can differentiate her baby's various cries after exposure.[139] A mother possesses a maternal instinct to recognize her toddler's desire, her teenager's pain, and her adult

---

[139] Bouchet, et al. (2020). Baby cry recognition is independent of motherhood but improved by experience and exposure. *The Royal Society of Publishing.*

child's silent need. How do mothers identify this? They have spent a considerable amount of time with their child. Conversely, a kid learns early how to get what he or she wants. Older children discern when it is safe to approach dad, and what their mom expects by a certain expression.

This concept is no different in our connection with our Heavenly Father. If we desire to understand God's will for our lives, we must "hang out" with Him—a lot. We have acquaintances, friends, and family, but only a select few are granted access to our hearts—the people we dare to be vulnerable with and share our deepest truths. THAT is the relationship we need to have with Jesus. Not just a Sunday morning acquaintance or family we visit a few times a week. God desires to be like that companion who you text constantly, call all the time, spend hours and hours with, and never want the time to end. The more the Lord becomes your confidant, the less you'll have to *pray* for God's will, because you'll just recognize it. The more we spend time with Jesus, the more our values shift to align with His. We begin to desire what He desires and want only what He wants.

DAILY STORY:

My own journey to drawing closer to the Lord came at a Teen Challenge event. I had been ministering there for twenty years, but this was the first time I was able to attend their annual BBQ (and the brisket was great!). But it wasn't my physical body that needed to be fed, but my spirit. This particular BBQ was special, because it was their 50th anniversary, and they were handing out anniversary copies of *The Cross & the Switchblade* by David Wilkerson. Now, I'm a sucker for any book, so I read it, not realizing the impact it would have on my life.

In 1958, David Wilkerson was watching TV when the Holy Spirit stirred inside him. David thought, "How much time do I spend in front of that screen each night...what would happen, Lord, if I sold that TV set and spent that time praying?"[140]

Each night after, instead of watching the television, he prayed. During one session, his eyes were drawn to *Life Magazine* on his desk. He tried to ignore it

---

[140] Wilkerson, D. (2018). *The cross and the switchblade.* Berkley Press.

because, of course, he was trying to pray. But the Holy Spirit kept nudging him to look, and when he did, it changed his life and soon millions. Overcome with compassion for teenagers on trial, he made a trip to New York. It was from that encounter that Wilkerson would create Teen Challenge two years later. (If you are unfamiliar with Teen Challenge, it is a faith-based program that helps people of all ages deal with addictions by introducing them to the power of forgiveness and freedom found in Jesus Christ.) According to Global Teen Challenge there are now 1,400 locations globally, in 140 countries, that save about 1,000 people per day. [141]

David didn't have to pray for *God's will*; he simply had to be available to listen to what the Lord was saying. His story became my story in that I turned off the TV and started praying. This challenge comes out of that story. So, his story and my story is now your story. What might God do in and through you?

---

[141] Global Teen Challenge. Until all live free.

Some people wonder how one hears the voice of God. Like David being nudged to read the *LIFE* magazine, the more I prayed, the more I discerned the Lord's desires for my life. Peace began to trail the answers I sought. He drew me to scriptures that spoke to questions in my heart, and He brought people to confirm His words. But...I could never have known His voice if I never talked to Him. Jesus said, "My sheep listen to my voice, and I know them, and they follow me..."[142]

The closer you get to God, the more He will speak to you and guide you to your purpose. His plans become your plans. His will becomes your will.

---

[142] John 10:27

REFLECTION: Read the scriptures listed above, then reflect on them below. Pick out keywords, verses, and themes. Write down how those might apply to your life.

Looking at the scriptures, pull out the words that demonstrate how we find God's will. During these 22 days, is there something God is starting to tell you? Write it down.

_____

_____

_____

_____

_____

_____

_____

_____

_____

_____

_____

_____

Matchbook

_____
_____
_____
_____
_____
_____
_____
_____
_____
_____
_____
_____
_____
_____
_____
_____
_____
_____
_____
_____
_____
_____
_____

PRAYER: Lord, I pray that you help me to submit to your will, to hear your voice, and surrender my life to you. Amen.

WRITE YOUR OWN PRAYER:

_____

_____

_____

_____

_____

_____

_____

_____

_____

_____

_____

_____

_____

_____

_____

_____

_____

TODAY'S CHALLENGE: Turn off everything, tune it all out, and find a place and time designated only for you and Jesus. Don't rush this time. Read your Bible, pray, worship, whatever it takes to get you to just rest in His presence. If you do this daily, eventually God will begin to speak to you, and you will build that intimate relationship to know His will without even asking.

🔥 DAY 23 🔥

Tending to the Fire

You see that his faith and
his actions were working together,
and his faith was made complete by what He did.
(James 2:22, NIV)

" … take the first step in faith,
even when you [can] not see the whole stairway,
and to leave the stairway to God"
(Marian W. Edelman, Rights Advocate with MLKJ)

DAILY READING:

James 2:14-26; Hebrews 6:10-12

DAILY THOUGHT:

If you walk away from a contained fire, it will likely go out on its own. In order to keep it burning, someone has to poke the logs and add more fuel when needed—in essence, they have to *do* something to keep it lit.

Walking is an *action*. If we say we are "walking in faith," then an *action* should be involved. As scripture says, faith without works is dead. [143] A harsh but true statement. Becoming a Christian is free and easy. We confess our sins, and He comes into our lives. We get baptized, find a church, and meet godly friends. We are good, but that is not where our faith in Christ stops. We are not supposed to merely sit in a pew, soaking in God's presence. We are called to more.

TODAY'S STORY

Imagine for a moment that you are excited to go on a trip with your friends across the globe. You brag to everyone you know. You dream about the food you want to try, the places you hope to visit, and the people you get to meet. Then, the day comes to leave, and you realize something awful. In all your busyness, you never bought a plane ticket.

---

[143] James 2:14

This is how a lot of Christians live their spiritual lives. We talk a good game about God's plan and purpose for our lives, but we never do anything to prepare for that plan and purpose. I have discovered, Jesus will not open a door if we are not ready to step through it.[144] He loves us too much.

We know by scripture that Jesus knew His calling by age twelve.[145] He didn't spend the next eighteen years doing nothing. He learned scripture.[146] He prayed. He prepared, so much so, that He baffled the teachers of the Law.[147] If God is calling you, are you getting the keys so when it is time, you can open the door? Or are you going to be the one who didn't buy the ticket? What training do you need? What group do you need to join? Who do you need to call? Where do you need to apply?

You cannot step into God's purpose if you do not have the right tools. You can't say God is calling you

---

[144] I Corinthians 3:10
[145] Luke 2:49-50
[146] II Timothy 3:15
[147] John 7:15

to be a nurse if you aren't enrolled in nursing school. So, if you are called to be a pastor, enroll in a Bible college or seminary. If you are called to be a missionary, start taking language lessons. If you are called to teach, go to college. If you're called to be in a triathlon to raise money for a ministry, then you need to start running.

No matter the calling, you have to do *your* part. That is obedience. As mentioned before, faith without works is dead.[148] Faith alone is not enough. What do you need to do today? Get your ticket, grab your keys, prepare your heart... be ready when the time arrives.

---

[148] James 2:26

REFLECTION: Read the scriptures listed above, then reflect on them below. Pick out keywords, verses, and themes. Write down how those might apply to your life.

What can I do to prepare for His calling, so that when it happens, I am ready? Write down your calling. Now, write down what it would take to get there. Then write down why you haven't started yet.

_____

_____

_____

_____

_____

_____

_____

_____

_____

_____

_____

_____

_____

_____

Matchbook

PRAYER: Lord, I pray that you help me to submit to your will, to hear your voice, and surrender my life to you. Amen.

WRITE YOUR OWN PRAYER:

_____

_____

_____

_____

_____

_____

_____

_____

_____

_____

_____

_____

_____

_____

_____

_____

_____

TODAY'S CHALLENGE: Whatever you need to do… I challenge you to apply or contact someone about that school, that group, etc. Whatever you need to do, to start the process. Don't wait. The time is now.

⚡ **DAY 24** ⚡

Striking Elsewhere

You intended to harm me,
but God intended it for good
to accomplish what is now being done,
the saving of many lives.
(Genesis 50:20, NIV)

"…we walk in a light which glorifies everything upon
which it falls, and turns losses into gains"
(Charles Spurgeon, 19th Century Preacher).

DAILY READING:

Psalm 9; Genesis 50:15-20

DAILY THOUGHT:

Have you ever tried to strike a match at the beach or on a windy day? My son and I decided to go for a picnic in the snow. We brought charcoal, hotdogs, and found an unoccupied fire pit at the site. But every time we tried to light a fire in the pit, the wind blew it out. After using half the matchbook, we shifted to a small grill that was covered on three sides. One strike and we were able to start our fire. It wasn't as fun as a campfire, but it still worked for cooking our food.

Detours to our plans aren't fun, but sometimes they are necessary for God's will to occur. If anyone understood detours, Joseph in the Bible did. His entire life was one big detour, from being sold into slavery by his brothers and being thrown into jail for false accusations. All of this was necessary, however, for Joseph to save thousands of lives.[149]

Detours can be painful. They are typically frustrating. But they are necessary. I like to think of it this way. God is in the helicopter, and we are in the car. His bird's eye view makes sense. The detour is for our own good. But if we ignore it, we can fall into a deep ditch. So, we have to trust Him.

---

[149] Genesis 47:13-26

DAILY STORY:

Before I went in the U.S. Army, I trained with a hardcore Marine. I was in shape and ready to go, but in order to get into basic training, I had to be able to demonstrate a single male push-up. No worries. I had been training for months. I climbed up on the table and got into the "front leaning rest position" (where the body is rigid, straight from head to heels, and arms and legs are shoulder length apart).

The woman drill sergeant said, "Go." I lowered myself down and up. "Lower," she snapped. I tried again. "Lower." Again. "Lower." Each time I went down and up, she said the same thing, "Lower." Pretty soon I had pushed out a dozen push-ups and yet, she still screamed, "Lower." Finally, my skinny arms wore out, and I dropped to the table. "Fit Co," she snapped. (Fit Co. was where the "out of shape" soldiers went to "die"...metaphorically speaking, of course.) It was eight hours of physical training a day. The drill sergeants "dropped" me to do push-ups for every little thing they could. "You looked at me funny. Drop and give me twenty." Or "I hear you were last in the chow line, drop and give me thirty." Or "Your shoelace is out of your boot. Drop and give me ten." Hours and hours we were left to painful, grueling exercise. But, by week two, I was able to complete *fifty* standard male push-ups.

As great as that sounds, I started boot camp two weeks late. All my new friends I'd met on the airplane entered basic training without me. I had to begin again with strangers in a fresh unit. But eventually, I graduated, and that snafu seemed a distant memory. That is, until I arrived at my school for technical training. But, as you may have guessed, I was two weeks late—so I had to wait for the next class to start. Again, I was frustrated until I learned that the entire class I was *supposed* to be in, shipped out to Panama for Operation Just Cause. I didn't, because I was two weeks late.

I graduated from Chaplain School and arrived at my permanent station. But, again, I was two weeks late, so they put another soldier in my spot. That "spot" was the first in our battalion to leave for Desert Storm. I didn't go—*at all*. A single push-up saved me from two wars.

Six months before, I was angry I couldn't do that one man's push-up. I questioned God. "Why did you bring me here and not help me pass?" But the Lord knew. He protected me. The detour was for *my* benefit.

We need to trust the Lord, even in the detour. You never know what the redirect will do in your favor. Detours may take longer, but remember—you are still moving.

REFLECTION: Read the scriptures listed above, then reflect on them below. Pick out keywords, verses, and themes. Write down how those might apply to your life.

Write your own psalm starting with "I will give thanks to you Lord, with all my heart..." Think of the detours in your life and write down how they have been for your benefit.

_____

_____

_____

_____

_____

_____

_____

_____

_____

_____

_____

_____

_____

_____

_____

_____

_____

_____

_____

_____

_____

_____

_____

_____

_____

_____

_____

_____

_____

_____

_____

_____

_____

PRAYER: Lord, I thank you for waking up today. Thank you for all that you've blessed me with. Thank you for bringing me away from where I've been. Thank you for those who love me, and even for those who don't. I praise your name. Amen.

WRITE YOUR OWN PRAYER:

_____

_____

_____

_____

_____

_____

_____

_____

_____

_____

_____

_____

_____

_____

_____

_____

_____

TODAY'S CHALLENGE: The challenge today is to simply thank God for every single detour in your lifetime. Praise Him for the obstacles, the trials, and the tribulations. Focus on the works of His hands, rather than the frustration.

PART IV

MAINTAINING THE FLAME

"KNOW & GROW"

There is something satisfying when the friction of the phosphorus ignites the matchstick, turning it white. The flicker, the smell of sulfur, the sound of the strike— and we have a flame. This abrasion ignites the flame into existence. As the scripture says, **"iron sharpens iron."** The friction against worldly things will make our fires burn brighter. But keeping the fire burning is not always easy. We have to maintain the fire consistently, to keep the flame. Spiritually, this comes from maintaining our walks by tending them daily.

DR. KIM MENDOZA

"The touch of God is marked by tears...deep, soul-shaking tears, weeping...it comes when that last barrier is down, and you surrender yourself to health and wholeness."

(David Wilkerson, *The Cross & the Switchblade*)

🔥 DAY 25 🔥

Scorching the Chaff

Finally, brothers and sisters, whatever is true,
whatever is noble, whatever is right, whatever is pure,
whatever is lovely, whatever is admirable
—if anything is excellent or praiseworthy—
think about such things.
(Philippians 4:8, NIV)

"Would it appall you or delight you if Christ revealed
your thoughts? We unconsciously assume that our
outer, physical, visible actions are going to be
the basis for our judgment [but] God places the
emphasis on the inner, invisible actions of the mind."
(T. W. Hunt, Author of *The Mind of Christ*).

DAILY READING:

I Corinthians 2:6-16; I Samuel 16:7; Philippians 2:2-7

DAILY THOUGHT:

In the Bible, the word "chaff" (the dry husk of grain that is burned) symbolizes the wicked and worthless, which is contrasted by the "useful wheat."[150] As our spiritual fire grows, the debris in our lives must be burned away.

In 1896, author Charles M. Sheldon wrote a novel entitled In *His Steps: What Would Jesus Do?*[151] In 1993, his great-grandson, Garrett Sheldon, wrote a book called *What Would Jesus Do?* This contemporary retelling created a worldwide phenomenon that most likely created more Jesus merchandise than any other Christian book before it. If you were alive then, you may have had at least one bracelet, bookmark, keychain, or sticker that touted the infamous—WWJD. Understanding what Jesus would do in most situations is hard to imagine. To fully grasp God's plan in a fallen world without a kingdom mindset is almost impossible. However, we are called to have a mind that is

---

[150] Matthew 3:12

[151] Diepenbrock, G. (2015). Book traces origin of phrase in WWJD movement to Topeka minister. *KU News*.

transformed and seeks after God above all else.[152] In truth, as for what Jesus would do: He'd wash the feet of Judas, even knowing the disciple would betray Him.

DAILY STORY:

One interesting story had a tragic beginning, but a remarkable ending. In 2006, at the West Nickel Mine one-room schoolhouse in Pennsylvania, a shooter entered a room full of Amish kids and shot them all before shooting himself. Instead of hating the shooter's mother, the Amish, with profound forgiveness, visited the shooter's family to offer comfort and compassion.[153] Some even attended his funeral to support the mother in her loss. This is the compassion and forgiveness that Jesus would give.

So, let's break down the actions of Jesus. If we follow His activities in the Gospels, we discover the mindset of Christ:

    1. He loves and cares for <u>everyone</u>.[154]

---

[152] Romans 12:2

[153] Glor, J. (2013, December). *Mother of Amish school shooter shares amazing story of forgiveness*. CBS News.

[154] Mark 1:41; Matthew 9:39; Matthew 14:14; John 3:16; Romans 5:8-9

2. He values all people.[155]
3. He forgives even those who hurt Him.[156]
4. He consistently sought time for isolated prayer because quality time spent with the Father was invaluable to Him.[157]
5. He told others about God and quoted scripture regularly in various situations, showing that He knew the Word.[158]
6. He had strong faith and acted on it.[159]
7. He sought to do God's will no matter what it cost Him personally.[160]

So how do we develop a mind of Christ? We work on these practices:

1. We love all people, even our enemies.
2. We believe in the inherent value of every individual, regardless of differences.

---

[155] Luke 19:1-10; John 8:1-11; John 4; Luke 17:11-19; Luke 7:36-50; Mark 5:21-43
[156] Luke 5:20; Luke 23:34; Matthew 18:21-22
[157] Matthew 14:23; Mark 1:35; Luke 5:16
[158] Matthew 4:4-10; 5:21, 27; Luke 7:27; Mark 12:36; John 15:25; Luke 23:46; Matthew 21:16
[159] Hebrews 12:2; Matt. 17:14-21
[160] Matthew 6:10; Matthew 7:21; Matthew 26:39

3. We forgive family members, friends, co-workers, and our enemies, no matter how they hurt us.

4. We set aside quality time daily to pray with the Lord.

5. We read our Bibles so that we know the Word of God well, and so that the Holy Spirit can speak to us.

6. We develop confidence and trust in the Holy Spirit by acting in faith.[161]

7. Above all, we seek to do God's will no matter what He asks of us.

This is how we develop a mind of Christ. We follow His example and do what He would do—love, pray, seek, and do.

---

[161] James 2:14-26

REFLECTION: Read the scriptures listed above, then reflect on them below. Pick out keywords, verses, and themes. Write down how those might apply to your life.

Really reflect on the seven things that we're to do in order to be like Jesus.

_____

_____

_____

_____

_____

_____

_____

_____

_____

_____

_____

_____

_____

_____

_____

_____

_____

PRAYER: Lord, help me to have a kingdom mindset. Give me the ability to follow after You in all that I do. Amen.

WRITE YOUR OWN PRAYER:

_____

_____

_____

_____

_____

_____

_____

_____

_____

_____

_____

_____

_____

_____

_____

_____

_____

_____

TODAY'S CHALLENGE: Looking at the seven actions above, determine which is the hardest for you, and then act on it.

♨ DAY 26 ♨

Ensuring the Burn

For if, by the trespass of the one man, death reigned through that one man, how much more will those who receive God's abundant provision of grace and of the gift of righteousness reign in life through the one man, Jesus Christ!
(Romans 5:17, NIV)

"Pray and let God worry."
(Martin Luther, 16th Century Theologian)

DAILY READING:

I Peter 5:1-11; Job 42:2; Proverbs 19:21

DAILY THOUGHT:

Did you know that if you *over*-tend a fire, you can smother it or cause it to become unstable? We need to trust the process and not get impatient, or our fire could die.

Have you ever heard the expression, "I told God my plans, and He just laughed." Often our plans are not His. We have to let go of the "reins." Interesting that the strips of leather that lead a horse are called "reins." When a cowboy holds the straps, he "reins" the horse's direction, and in the same vein, if we let go (handing over the reins), we allow God to take control (reign) and guide the direction of our lives.

DAILY STORY:

I am notorious for trying to make things happen on my own. Waiting is painful. Many supervisors have said, *"Grass never grows beneath Kimberlee."* As you can imagine, this gets me in trouble—often. After two years of trying to get my dream job, I shared my frustration with my family. Each member, one by one, said, "I've never had to apply for a job, God just gives them to me." Crying, I said, "Well, that has never happened to me." My stepdad paused and said,

"That's because *you* are always the one trying to make things happen."

Ouch! But he was right. I never gave God time to work. I pressed forward and attempted to make the situation morph into my dream, my desire. At one point, I felt God say I'd be a full-time professor, and therefore, *I* was going to do whatever I needed to do to make that happen. The problem was, it would happen in *His* timing, not by my manipulation of the situation. Now, don't get me wrong, acting in faith is important—but attempting to control the situation is not. I call it "the wall." Let me give you an example:

My oldest son had recently gotten married but couldn't afford to rent a place in San Diego (where we were living at the time). So, my husband and I decided to build a small studio apartment on the back of our property. First, we needed a loan. Usually, this process happened fast. But no matter what we did, we just couldn't get one. Finally, we determined as a family that we weren't going to push through this "wall" and trust God. Had we kept trying, my next story would not have been possible.

At one point, I had five schools in Texas interview me. One of those was Wayland Baptist University in the Texas Panhandle. I turned them down because *I* wanted to live in East Texas. In all four interviews, it was just me and one other person—and they picked the other person.

In jest I said, "I bet I was supposed to go to Wayland." Now, I might have been joking, but the Lord was not. The next day, the Vice President of Academics called and asked, "Are you sure you don't want to come to Wayland?"

My appointment in the Panhandle has been nothing short of miraculous. I recognize the purpose that brought me here. If I had kept pushing the "wall" to acquire *my* agenda, I would have missed out on so much that the Lord had for me and others. Had I obtained a loan on my home for my son's apartment, we wouldn't have had the equity to buy our new home and my son a home in Texas. In obedience, it worked out better. I've seen lives changed and discovered my true calling. A female prayer warrior once told me, "I bet God's plan isn't going to look anything like you think it will." Boy was that "word" prophetic. It didn't, and I thank God for that.

We have to be careful about trying to create our own miracles. Let's consider Abraham and Sarah. God promised Abraham he would have descendants as vast as the stars.[162] But the impatient couple took matters into their own hands. Abraham slept with his slave Hagar, who gave birth to Ishmael.[163] This one decision has caused a continuous religious war of unimaginable magnitude for more than a millennia in the Middle East. Why? Because most believe Ismael is the seed of Islam, and Sarah's son, Isaac, is the seed of Israel.[164] Hundreds of thousands of people have died due to this on-going conflict. All because one couple didn't *trust* God and felt they needed to "move things along."

Like Abraham and Sarah, we often try to manipulate a path to go around our wall, when God has another

---

[162] Genesis 15:5
[163] Genesis 16
[164] Jacobson, (2023); The Israel Team (n.d.)

door designed for us. We must surrender our timetable to God and let Him guide us. Reader, if you get nothing else in these forty days, realize that God's way is *always* the right one. We have to allow Him to take charge. In the end, you will understand—and it will be amazing! But if we fail to follow His path, either He will use someone else or something bad might happen. Trust God. He's a good God. He's got you.

REFLECTION: Read the scriptures listed above, then reflect on them below. Pick out keywords, verses, and themes. Write down how those might apply to your life.

Write down all the walls in your life right now. Reflect on if you are pushing against them or letting God direct you?

_____

_____

_____

_____

_____

_____

_____

_____

_____

_____

_____

_____

_____

PRAYER: Lord, help me to let you reign in every area of my life. Take control and direct my path. Amen.

WRITE YOUR OWN PRAYER:

_____

_____

_____

_____

_____

_____

_____

_____

_____

_____

_____

_____

_____

_____

_____

_____

_____

TODAY'S CHALLENGE: It's simple. Let go of the reins, stop pushing the wall, totally surrender and let God design and lead your path.

⚜ **DAY 27** ⚜

Staying Near the Fire

For everyone born of God overcomes the world.
This is the victory that has overcome
the world, even our faith.
(I John 5:4, NIV)

"Obstacles are those frightful things you see when
you take your eyes off your goal."
(Henry Ford, Industrialist)

DAILY READING:

John 16; Matthew 24

DAILY THOUGHT:

If you have ever been camping on a cold night, you know how it is when you move away from the fire to go to the restroom or your tent. It's nice to stay near the heat. In addition, critters and bugs are less likely to bother you near the fire. So, in essence, staying near the fire keeps you warm and safe. In this metaphor, the space away from the fire is the world. The fire is God. We need to stay close to the fire to be protected and fiery in our faith.

Jesus left this earth almost 2,000 years ago. The situation in Israel was far from godly and peaceful. There was social, political, and religious unrest: Extreme poverty, judgmental religious leaders, corrupt politicians, and division and prejudice among the various people groups. Do any of these issues sound familiar? The Jewish people in 30 C.E. understood chaos and worldly issues. Yet, Jesus said to fear not, for He has overcome the world.[165] If that sentiment was true then, it is still true today. We do not need to fear, for Jesus is greater than anything that we glimpse in the news or experience in our neighborhoods. He is not subject to *any* earthly ruler and has a solution to your problem beyond anything you can envision.

---

[165] John 16:33

DAILY STORY:

About a year or so ago, I became a YouTube addict. I found the news horrifying, but I couldn't stop watching it. I viewed… Horrendous shootings. Vicious fires. Tremendous floods. Devastating wars. Threats of hostilities towards our country. Pastors falling from grace. Ugly rhetoric from both sides of the political aisle. Vile stories of the Hollywood elite. An increase in disease, sex trafficking, and abuse. Frightening videos on the end times. Ministers bad mouthing other ministers. And that was only one Saturday.

I found all of it made me sick at night. In full transparency, these stories kept me from spending quality time with the Lord. As much as they alarmed me, I craved more, like one craves the next soap opera episode. I started to get drawn into conspiracies and became overwhelmed by the future. No matter what, even though I sensed God telling me to stop, I just wouldn't.

One day, I felt called to finish this book. I agreed to do another forty-days without TV or YouTube. I spent that time just soaking in God's presence. My eyes were opened, and for once, I could see the chaos for what it was—"conforming to the pattern of this world," and I was needing to renew my mind.[166]

Are you getting drawn in yourself? Do you fear the things around you? These stories I watched may be the "birth pains" prophesied in the Bible thousands of years ago, which means...God is not surprised.[167] In fact, there is nothing that happens on this earth that God does not allow. He is in control. The madness may seem terrifying, especially since we don't know how much worse it will get before Jesus returns or we pass away. Focusing on the chaos can frighten us. That's why we need to keep our eyes focused on the one who wins in the end. Jesus has overcome death and the grave. [168] He has overcome the sinful nature of mankind, sickness, poverty, destruction, and pain. There is nothing you are enduring (or will endure) that Jesus cannot support you through. We are not called

---

[166] Romans 12:2
[167] Matthew 24:8
[168] I Corinthians 15:54-57

to *worry*; we are called to *trust* Jesus.[169] The Bible states, "The LORD himself goes before you and will be with you; he will never leave you nor forsake you..."[170]

When scripture prophesies the destruction of our world, Joel finished by saying, "And everyone who calls on the name of the Lord will be saved."[171] In addition, the Bible talks about wonderful promises, too.[172] It states that God's Spirit will pour out on all people. People will prophesy, see visions, and dream dreams. The world will experience wonders and signs. Have confidence that God has a plan. He is still here, in our midst, calling us to be strong and on fire for Him until the day of His return.[173]

---

[169] Philippians 4:6-7
[170] Deuteronomy 31:8
[171] Joel 2:32
[172] Acts 2:17-21
[173] Matthew 24:44

REFLECTION: Read the scriptures listed above, then reflect on them below. Pick out keywords, verses, and themes. Write down how those might apply to your life.

Write down your fears. What do you need to do to move past them?

_____

_____

_____

_____

_____

_____

_____

_____

_____

_____

_____

_____

_____

_____

Matchbook

PRAYER: Lord, help me to focus completely on you, so that my heart is aligned with you, and I have no external worries. Amen.

WRITE YOUR OWN PRAYER:

_____
_____
_____
_____
_____
_____
_____
_____
_____
_____
_____
_____
_____
_____
_____
_____

TODAY'S CHALLENGE: You wrote down your fears and things that you can do to move past them. You cannot get past a fear until you face it straight on. Take a step of faith and make that first move.

�🔥 DAY 28 🔥

Focusing on the Flames

"My presence will go with you,
and I will give you rest"
(Exodus 33:14, NIV).

"It takes practice to become proficient at something.
Practicing the presence of God
will make us good at it."
(R. Alan Woods, Christian Author)

DAILY READING:

Psalm 91

DAILY THOUGHT:

While sitting by a campfire, I love watching the dancing flames. Without the distractions of cell phones and computers (because they usually don't work in the woods) it is relaxing to have a moment to enjoy nature, watching the fire, without talking, just thinking.

Today, I dare you to turn on a timer and just sit in God's presence for twenty minutes, not praying, just praising Him and waiting for Him to speak into your heart. We need to get out of our minds, let go of distractions, and just soak in Him. Listen to God as you spend time with Him. If you find your mind wandering, just write that thing down in your journal, and try again. Of course, when you try to do this, the phone will ring, the kids will come in, the spouse will start hammering, the dog will start barking… the enemy will inevitably try to distract you. But don't let him or anything take you out of God's presence. This is spiritual warfare. The Bible states that our struggle is not against flesh and blood but against the powers and spiritual forces of this dark world. [174] Not all spiritual warfare is "doing." The enemy loves to use the weapons of distraction. But our greatest weapon is in the silence. We benefit spiritually when we rest in the Lord. We find peace, rest, and joy when our day is not all cluttered;

---

[174] Ephesians 6:12

we find time to dwell in the manifestation of the Holy Spirit.

DAILY STORY:

For years, I struggled with anxiety. I am Type "A" times twenty. My mind does not shut down easily. I started having panic attacks for no reason. So, I went to the doctor to get help. My doctor said, "Get off technology and start to meditate one hour before you go to bed. This will help you relax and sleep better." (Of course, I interpreted "meditation" as "prayer.") Time spent with God not only benefits our spiritual life but is a holistic endeavor. It quiets our minds, relaxes our bodies, and brings our spiritual hearts into alignment with God's—mind, body, and spirit. Putting this hour into practice, I noticed my anxiety lessened. I slept better. I acted better. I experienced more joy. I felt more peace.

I may not be a *medical* doctor, but I am a "doctor," and I "prescribe" this—get in God's presence and watch how much better you feel.

REFLECTION: Read the scriptures listed above, then reflect on them below. Pick out keywords, verses, and themes. Write down how those might apply to your life.

Write down what you need to release. Let everything go (write it down if you need to get it out of your head) and just wait on the Lord in His Presence. He has something to show you.

_____

_____

_____

_____

_____

_____

_____

_____

_____

_____

_____

_____

_____

_____

_____

_____

_____

_____

_____

_____

_____

_____

_____

_____

_____

_____

_____

_____

_____

_____

_____

_____

_____

PRAYER: Lord, help me to know when to act and when to rest in you. Give me the wisdom and strength to release my life and abilities into your hands. Let me stop thinking and just release in your presence. Amen.

WRITE YOUR OWN PRAYER:

_____

_____

_____

_____

_____

_____

_____

_____

_____

_____

_____

_____

_____

_____

TODAY'S CHALLENGE: Today is all about just sitting in God's presence. Turn off the phone. Close the computer. Maybe turn on some worship music, and for thirty minutes, make it about you and God.

🔥 **DAY 29** 🔥

Lighting a Torch

Have I not commanded you? Be strong and
courageous. Do not be afraid.
do not be discouraged,
for the LORD your God will be with you
wherever you go.
(Joshua 1:9, NIV)

"Fear is only as powerful as the attention you give it."
(Glody Kikonga, Author of *Mental Toughness*)

DAILY THOUGHT:

When camping, one of the scariest moments for me is
when I have to amble through the dark forest to use
the restroom. So, I always take the brightest flashlight
with me. In ancient days, I would have had to light a
torch from my fire and carry a flame with me.

Like the days of old, when we move into the darkness, we shouldn't be afraid, because we carry the light with us. As scripture points out, light always overcomes the darkness, not the other way around.[175]

Can you imagine being Esther in the Bible?[176] She was a young Jewish virgin, taken into the King's harem. Somehow, she won his favor, and he made her Queen. Now, the King had the power to save or kill a person by a simple gesture of the movement of his scepter. If he held it out, the person could live. If not, the person would die. No one was immune to this, even the Queen. After all, Queen Vashti, (the Queen before Esther) was likely executed just for refusing to attend a banquet. Read the full story (in today's reading). You will see that the stakes were high. But Queen Esther stepped out of her comfort zone in order to save God's people. God will call us to great but sometimes daunting places. However, He will never call us without giving us the tools.

---

[175] John 1:5
[176] Esther 1-10

DAILY STORY:

Probably the scariest thing I've ever done is accept a position as a school dean at a Christian university. Up until that point, I had only been a director. Ever heard of *imposter syndrome*? (It's where a person persistently believes he or she doesn't belong where he or she is, and that there must be some mistake, because he or she couldn't possibly have deserved it or had the skills.) Well, when I was offered the job, I had a big case of *imposter syndrome*. Not only that, but I had a month to move from California to Texas to start the job. Everything in me screamed, "What am I doing? Can I even do this?" But God did not bring me to the high plains of Texas just to desert me. He had me. He provided me with what I needed and more.

As I edit this, a young adult named Haven comes to mind. Her very name means a "place of safety." When I first met Haven, she was a shy girl who hoped I would call on someone else. But God has a call on her life. In an effort to be obedient, I've watched her step out in faith. Only a year later, she sings on the worship team, speaks out when God gives her a word, prays for others, and is leading a Bible study. I could not be prouder of her.

There are people dying without Jesus. We cannot hold onto our place of safety and let them fall off a cliff. We need to trust God in our calling. No matter what God brings you to, He will help you through it. He is a good God. A loving God. He sees you. Now take that step. He's got hold of you.

REFLECTION: Read the scriptures listed above, then reflect on them below. Pick out keywords, verses, and themes. Write down how those might apply to your life.

Do you have imposter syndrome? Consider all the people (and God) who have told you that you are skilled in a specific area and reflect on that.

_____

_____

_____

_____

_____

_____

_____

_____

_____

_____

_____

_____

_____

_____

_____

_____

_____

_____

_____

_____

_____

_____

_____

_____

_____

_____

_____

_____

_____

_____

_____

_____

_____

_____

_____

_____

_____

_____

PRAYER: Lord, give me the courage to step out of my comfort zone. Provide all I need. Amen.

WRITE YOUR OWN PRAYER:

_____

_____

_____

_____

_____

_____

_____

_____

_____

_____

_____

_____

_____

_____

_____

_____

TODAY'S CHALLENGE: Whatever it is, you know what it is, take that crazy step out of the comfort zone and into God's glorious plan.

🔥 **DAY 30** 🔥

Containing the Heat

I am the good shepherd.
The good shepherd lays down
his life for the sheep.
(John 10:11, NIV)

"There's a difference between knowing God
and knowing about God. When you truly know God,
you have energy to serve Him, boldness to share
Him, and contentment in Him."
(J.I. Packer, Author of *Knowing God*)

DAILY READING:

II Samuel 22; and the scriptures in the reading listed below.

DAILY THOUGHT:

As mentioned a few times before, stepping away from the heat of the fire can be uncomfortable. But there are times when we must. Maybe to fetch some more wood. Maybe to grab another marshmallow. Whatever the reason, if we've been near the fire long enough, the heat stays with us as we step away a short distance. If we are near the fire (Jesus) long enough, the warmth of His spirit stays with us no matter where we go.

We can know *of* people but not know them intimately. Knowing *of* Jesus, even calling yourself a "Christian," does not mean you have an intimate relationship with Him. It's like me saying I am friends with Evangeline Lilly because I shared an elevator ride with her once. What turns an acquaintance into a friend? Quality time with the other person. The more time we spend in Christ's presence, the more we *actually* know Him.

Who is Jesus? He is...

- **Alpha & Omega** (Revelation 22:13)
- **Author & Perfecter of our faith** (Hebrews 12:2)

- **Bread of Life** (John 6:35)
- **Bridegroom** (Matthew 9:15)
- **Christ (Matthew 16:15-17)**
- **Cornerstone** (Acts 4:11)
- **Deliverer** (Romans 11:26)
- **Faithful & True** (Revelation 19:11)
- **Good Shepherd** (John 10:11)
- **Head of the Church** (Ephesians 1:22)
- **High Priest** (Hebrews 4:14)
- **I am** (John 8:58)
- **Immanuel** (Matthew 1:23)
- **King of Kings** (Revelation 19:16)
- **Lamb** (Revelation 17:14)
- **Lamb of God** (John 1:29)
- **Light of this World** (John 8:12)
- **Lion of Judah** (Revelation 5:5)
- **Lord** (Romans 10:9)
- **Messiah** (John 4:25-26)
- **Morning Star** (Revelation 22:16)
- **Peace** (Ephesians 2:14)
- **Rock** (I Corinthians 10:4)
- **Savior** (Luke 2:11)
- **Servant** (Acts 4:30)

- **Son of God** (I John 5:20)
- **Son of the Most High** (Luke 1:31)
- **The Way** (John 14:6)
- **The Word** (John 1:1)
- **Truth** (John 8:32)

Sheep are easily distracted and have poor eyesight. For this reason, it is important that they can discern their master's voice. When he calls, they come. They understand that the shepherd offers guidance, provides protection, and leads them to green pastures (e.g. provision). When strangers call, sheep will not go with them. I'm sure you can see the imagery. We too are distracted. We often have poor vision when it comes to the future or spiritual things. We need to know the Master's voice, so He can provide, guide, and protect us from an enemy who would love to lead us astray.[177] We need to know our Shepherd.

DAILY STORY:

I met a couple who prays the various names of God over whatever they need in prayer. For instance, if I

---

[177] John 10:11

say that my back is hurting, they will pray, "Jehovah Rapha (*The Lord who Heals*), heal her back." If I said I need money to pay a bill, they would pray, "Jehovah Jireh (*The Lord who Provides*), please provide the funds to pay this bill." I found this fascinating, so I asked about it.

I was told that each name reveals an attribute of God's character. This helps personalize the prayer, aligning it with God's specific trait. God has an abundance of resources and wisdom to help us with every situation and need. Here are just a few names for God the Father:

Abba—Papa (name of endearment)[178]
Adonai—Lord or Master[179]
Alpha & Omega—Beginning and the End[180]
Elohim—Creator[181]
El Elyon—The Most High[182]

---

[178] Galatians 4:6
[179] Judges 6:15
[180] Revelation 1:8
[181] Genesis 17:7
[182] Psalm 7:17

El Shaddai—God Almighty[183]

El Roi—The God who Sees Me[184]

Jehovah Jireh—The Lord will Provide[185]

Jehovah Nissi—The Lord is my Banner (Victory)[186]

Jehovah Rapha—The Lord who Heals[187]

Jehovah Ro'i—The Lord our Shepherd[188]

Jehovah Shalom—The Lord our Peace[189]

Jehovah Shammah—The Lord is There[190]

Jehovah Tsidkenu—The Lord our Righteousness[191]

Yahweh (or Jehovah)—LORD[192]

Yahweh M'Kaddesh—The Lord who Makes Holy[193]

---

[183] Ruth 1:20
[184] Genesis 16:1-14
[185] Genesis 22:14
[186186] Exodus 17:15
[187] Exodus 15:26
[188] Psalm 23:1
[189] Judges 6:24
[190] Ezekiel 48:35
[191] Jeremiah 33:16
[192] Exodus 3:15
[193] Leviticus 20:8

REFLECTION: Read the scriptures listed above, then reflect on them below. Pick out keywords, verses, and themes. Write down how those might apply to your life.

Consider the list above and write down who He is most to you today.

_____

_____

_____

_____

_____

_____

_____

_____

_____

_____

_____

_____

_____

_____

_____

_____

PRAYER: Lord, thank you for who you are and the free gift of salvation. I pray I remember to call on you when I am in trouble or discouraged. Amen.

WRITE YOUR OWN PRAYER:

_____

_____

_____

_____

_____

_____

_____

_____

_____

_____

_____

_____

_____

_____

TODAY'S CHALLENGE: Reflect long and hard on how well you know Jesus. Do you know Him like an actual best friend? Like a parent? The key to knowing this is how long you can talk to Him. A good friend you can talk to for hours and not even realize it.

ᕙ DAY 31 ᕗ

Forging through the Flames

Yet you, LORD, are our Father.
We are the clay, you are the potter;
we are all the work of your hand.
(Isaiah 64:8, NIV)

As we place our dependence upon God, an
incredible freedom and peace will begin to rest
in our hearts. And reaching that point
in our lives makes every failure worth it."
(Charles Stanley, Author of *I Lift Up My Soul*)

DAILY READING:

Jeremiah 18:2-6; Job 10:8-12

DAILY THOUGHT:

Most people know that a healthy respect for fire is
necessary for safety. Someone who doesn't respect its

power can find themselves hurt or worse. Yet certain things only reach their potential when passed through the flames. In that heat, they are not destroyed, but sterilized, preserved, molded, and strengthened.

God is the supreme sculptor, and the human race is His ultimate sculpture.[194] From clay, He formed us.[195] Even now, He continues to shape us into beautiful works of art—if we let Him. Just as a potter kneads the clay to remove air bubbles in order to improve its workability and durability, God also kneads us. This process is necessary to prevent us from breaking and primes us for His plan. Once the sculpture is formed, it is placed in a kiln (an oven) to make the piece stronger. Similarly, there are times God allows us to go through the "fire." Though this kneading and fiery process can be painful, it fortifies us for the path ahead.

DAILY STORY:

I know I've mentioned Rev. David Wilkerson before, but I cannot think of a better story than this to illustrate

---

[194] Isaiah 64:8
[195] Genesis 2:7

my next point. When the pastor first set out to New York, he seriously thought God called him to help seven young gang members being held for capital murder.[196] But when he got to the courthouse, not only did the judge not let him see the young men, but David almost got arrested and was tossed out by the police. To add insult to injury, the newspapers caught a photo of it and published the story.

Talk about a slammed closed door. At the time, David felt confused. His town was shocked, and fellow pastors were angry at his stupidity. But David couldn't help the draw to New York. So, again, he drove the eight hours and tried to see the young men. Now, if you haven't read the story (which I highly encourage you to do), you're probably like, "So, here's where the doors open wide and the angels sing, right?" Wrong. David never met those boys.

Because God had other plans. Because David was tossed out of the courtroom by the cops, other gang

---

[196] Wilkerson, D. (2008). *The Cross & the Switchblade*. Berkley Press.

members started talking to him; in their minds, he was "one of them." This opened an unusual door. Likely, one he never would have achieved without the embarrassment of the news article. Instead of seven kids, he has now reached millions of lives.

Another story happened a few years ago at Asbury University. In 2023, the leadership coordinator for the missions organization, *Envision* preached at a morning chapel. At the end of the service, no one came forward. Discouraged, the pastor texted his wife: "Latest stinker. I'll be home soon."[197] What he didn't know was that the Holy Spirit was working. Students remained to pray after the service concluded, and they would continue to pray for two weeks. By the end, over 50,000 people had joined them.

Allowing God to mold us is another way of saying we trust Him in the forming process. We can't always see what the Holy Spirit is doing under the surface. Your situation may appear to be disconnected from any sort

---

[197] Silliman, D. (2023). No celebrities except Jesus: How Asbury protected the revival. *Christianity Today*.

of future—but eventually, it *will* make sense. When you're going through a trial, realize it might be God preparing you to help someone later. The skills learned in your odd job may benefit your future. Instead of complaining about the circumstance, yield to the Potter's hand.

REFLECTION: Read the scriptures listed above, then reflect on them below. Pick out keywords, verses, and themes. Write down how those might apply to your life.

Write who you were and who you are now. Where do you see the hand of God in your life?

_____

_____

_____

_____

_____

_____

_____

_____

_____

_____

_____

_____

_____

_____

_____

_____

_____

Matchbook

PRAYER: Lord, help me to see myself as you see me. Help me to begin to see and believe in the purpose you have for my life. May I also treat others in the same way, as we are all your creation, and deserve that respect. Amen.

WRITE YOUR OWN PRAYER:

_____

_____

_____

_____

_____

_____

_____

_____

_____

_____

_____

_____

_____

_____

_____

_____

_____

TODAY'S CHALLENGE: Draw your life in an abstract form. What does it look like? How would you explain it? What do you think God intends for that form? If you haven't asked Him yet, ask Him.

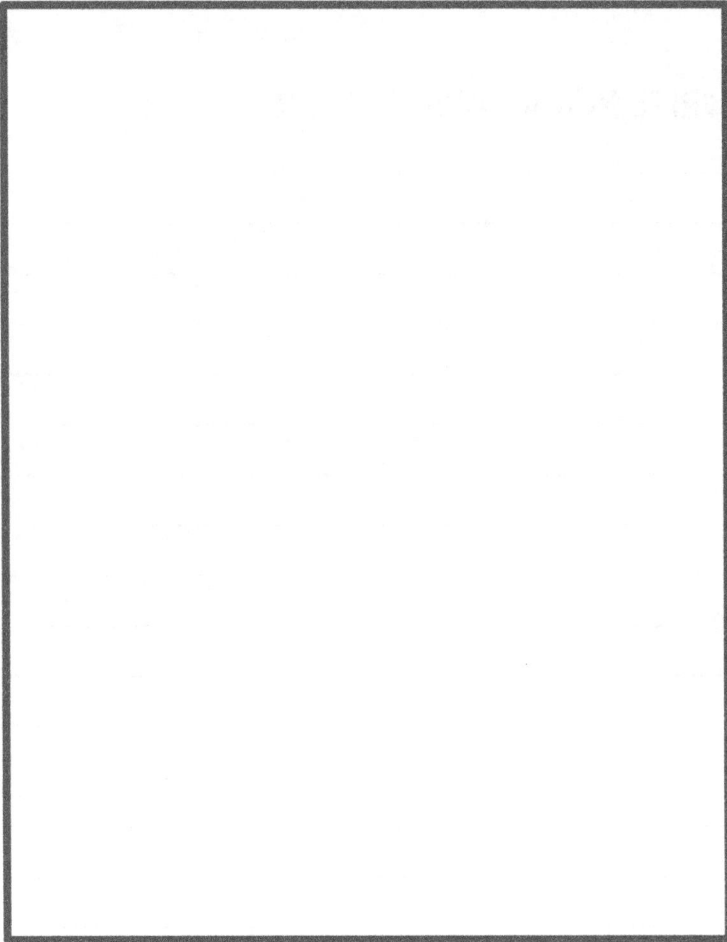

�🔥 DAY 32 🔥

Warming the Hands

Give thanks in all circumstances;
for this is the will of God in Christ Jesus for you.
(I Thessalonians 5:18, NIV)

"Life is 10% what happens to you
and 90% how you react to it."
(Charles R. Swindoll, Author and Pastor)

DAILY READING:

Psalm 150:1-6; Psalm 118:24; Colossians 3:17

DAILY THOUGHT:

When I'm "freezing," I am thankful for the fire. I rub my hands together and then put my palms out towards the flames. These two motions make me think of prayer and praise. A lot of this book so far has focused on prayer, but today I want to talk about praise and thanksgiving.

Thanksgiving is defined as "gratitude, especially to God" and *gratitude* is defined as "being grateful and wanting to <u>express</u> your thanks."[198] When we consider the Lord, we recognize He has given us everything, both here in the physical and for all eternity. While we were still sinners, He gave us His only Son so that we might have life.[199] True gratitude doesn't just feel thankful—it inspires us to give back. While we can never repay what Christ has done for us, we can strive to honor Him.

Often, we get caught up in the mundane and the insignificant. We become like the Israelites, complaining about our "manna." For example, we grumble about the song selections in church. We gripe about the message the pastor preached. We criticize the lack of programs in our church. In truth, we can be

---

[198] Gratitude. Oxford Learning Dictionaries. Retrieved from https://www.oxfordlearnersdictionaries.com/us/definition/american_english/grati tude#:~:text=noun-,noun,everyone%20for%20their%20hard%20work.
[199] Romans 5:8-9

slow to pause and contemplate how blessed the American Christian truly is. **Anyone who has ever been a missionary in a country facing religious persecution can attest to this.** Christians in those areas are so grateful for Jesus that they cling to every piece of Scripture they can find.[200]

DAILY STORY:

Recently, I read *When Faith is Forbidden* by The Voice of the Martyrs. Todd Nettleton shared testimony after testimony of worship and praise, despite the various stories of persecution. Christians in hostile locations thanked God for incarceration because they could readily share the Gospel without fear. They worshiped Jesus inside dank and dark cells. Some praised God after a whipping or maiming had occurred, awaiting the day they could share the Bible again.

In another book (sorry can't remember the name), I read about two Christian women who were locked up in an Iranian jail for giving away Bibles. The ladies didn't complain but rather rejoiced and praised Jesus

---

[200] Voice of the Martyrs. www.persecution.com.

for being placed where they could share the Gospel so freely. They made makeshift Bibles for the women from all the scriptures they could recall and passed them out. Though they were in prison, their calling would not be stopped.

Western societies sometimes forget the simplest of lessons—we have salvation, bought by the blood of our Lord Jesus Christ, and at the end of the day, that *is enough.* [201] I heard a pastor once say, "People complain about the worship songs, forgetting it's not about them."

The priority should always be worshiping God in *any situation*, with *any song*, under *any pastor*, in *any location*—no matter the situation. If we can be content and find joy in every circumstance, we are more likely to discover true gratitude.

---

[201] Ephesians 2:8-9

REFLECTION: Read the scriptures listed above, then reflect on them below. Pick out keywords, verses, and themes. Write down how those might apply to your life.

Write down all that God has done for you.

_____

_____

_____

_____

_____

_____

_____

_____

_____

_____

_____

_____

_____

_____

_____

_____

PRAYER: Lord, thank you for all that You have done in my life. I praise you. Amen.

WRITE YOUR OWN PRAYER:

_____

_____

_____

_____

_____

_____

_____

_____

_____

_____

_____

_____

_____

_____

_____

_____

_____

TODAY'S CHALLENGE: Consider one thing (or person) which annoys you. Now, spend time thinking about how that thing (or person) is a blessing. Then thank God for the thing (or person). If it is a person, start praying for him or her.

PART V

FANNING THE FLAMES

"PREPARE & SHARE"

We have made it to the final eight days of our journey. Hopefully, by this time, you are ignited and excited. This last section is meant to encourage you to fan those flames, so they will burn brighter. When a fire grows tall enough, others can see it from way off. That is what we are called to do. It is not enough to be on fire for the Lord. Our fire needs to spread. Revivals typically ignite with just a handful of people, but their momentum builds, and spreads like an unstoppable forest fire.

"Be who God meant
you to be,
and you will set
[the world] on fire."
(St. Catherine of Siena, 1376)

⚶ DAY 33 ⚶

Igniting Others

Never be ashamed to tell others about our Lord…
(*II Timothy 1:8*)

"The Father wants all to
come to repentance and so should we."
(Amir Tsarfati, Author & Speaker)

DAILY READING:

Matthew 28:16-20; John 4:1-38

DAILY THOUGHT:

Ignition is the point at which an item burns. It is in the spark. As we grow in our faith, we need to have the ability to spread our fire by igniting others.

After spending a lot of time on our own faith, we should share that faith. People like to brag about their new careers, children's successes, exciting vacations, and academic achievements, but how often do they brag about what God has done in their lives? Jeremiah writes that if we are to boast, we should only boast about the Lord.[202]

In truth, we have the answer to the world's pain and suffering. We need to share it. If God has done anything for you in the last 33 days, tell people. Ignite others to read the Word and pray more. Fire is contagious. Revival may start with one person, but it doesn't stay there. You may think that you cannot set such a fire, but I believe you can.

DAILY STORY:

There are millions of stories about how a few people started huge revivals. Here are just a few:

Eighteen Students—The Asbury University Revival started with a handful of young adults praying and ended with 50,000 people from around the globe.[203]

---

[202] Jeremiah 9:24

[203] Weissman, S. (2023). The aftershocks of the Asbury revival. *Inside Higher Ed.*

Twelve men—The Disciples were twelve men who prayed in unity and witnessed 3000-plus, people saved, not to mention the billions since.[204]

Two Men—Reverend Chuck Smith, along with Lonnie Frisbee, welcomed the hippies into the church and started a revival in Southern California that saved more than 250,000 people, not to mention the millions of lives those individuals have touched since.[205]

One Man—Reverend David Wilkerson turned off his television, prayed, and started Teen Challenge—an organization that now has more than 1,250 centers around the world, reaching over 1.1 million people in 2024 alone and approximately 7 million since 1958.[206]

One Woman—Mother Teresa left the comfort of her convent and followed God's charge to India. Her service and sacrifice to Christ have helped more

---

[204] Acts 2:41

[205] Whitman, A. (2023). Jesus revolution: The 60s hippies who changed the world. *Premier Christianity.*

[206] Teenchallengeusa.org

people than could ever be calculated. To this day, her charity operates 275 soup kitchens, 224 children's homes, 438 homes for the dying, with over 5,100 women now serving in her shadow.[207]

As *The Purpose Driven Life* starts, "It is not about you."[208] This challenge was never meant to just help *you*. It was meant to breathe fire back into the church and set the world ablaze. You've started the first part by praying daily. Now, it is time to take your faith to the next step and spread your testimony. Share the power of Jesus and the Holy Spirit with others. Who knows, you just might start a fire that cannot be contained. How awesome would that be?

---

[207] Towey, J. (2022). Mother Teresa and the sisters who stay. *Aging with Dignity*.
[208] Warren, R. (2002). *The purpose driven life*. Zondervan.

REFLECTION: Read the scriptures listed above, then reflect on them below. Pick out keywords, verses, and themes. Write down how those might apply to your life.

What has changed in your life in the last 33 days? Who can you tell? What action do you need to take to share your experience?

_____

_____

_____

_____

_____

_____

_____

_____

_____

_____

_____

_____

_____

DR. KIM MENDOZA

PRAYER: Dear Lord, reveal to me the people I need to speak to. Give me opportunities to share my testimony. Amen

WRITE YOUR OWN PRAYER:

_____

_____

_____

_____

_____

_____

_____

_____

_____

_____

_____

_____

_____

_____

_____

TODAY'S CHALLENGE: Call or write *a family member or friend who needs to hear your testimony.*

ᗯ DAY 34 ᗯ

Generating an Inferno

For no word from God will ever fail.
(Luke 1:37, NIV)

"Most of us don't get what we want because we quit praying. We give up too easily. We give up too soon. We quit praying right before the miracle happens." (Mark Batterson, Author of *The Circle Maker*)

DAILY READING:

Exodus 14; II Kings 20:1-6; Joshua 6:1-27; Mark 9:23

DAILY THOUGHT:

An inferno is an enormous, fierce fire. As we tend the fire of our hearts, it is hopefully going to burn bright. The Holy Spirit displayed His power like tongues of fire at Pentecost.[209] We see this same power occurring countless times in scripture.[210] Being on fire is great, but my hope for you is that your faith would be an inferno. A simple fire can die out easily, but an inferno catches others on fire. That level of fire comes through fervent faith and prayer.

The first two scripture readings for this week depict God splitting bodies of water. While the miracle of Moses splitting the Red Sea[211] is well-known, fewer people know the same event occurred twice more with Elisha and Elijah.[212] Same miracle on a smaller scale. What this demonstrates is… if God has done it once, God can do it again. If God has done it for someone else, God can do it for you.

We talked about Jericho[213] in Week 6, but I wanted to mention one more thing. The Lord told the people to march around seven times. What if they had stopped on the sixth time because they were too tired? Their

---

[209] Acts 2:1-4
[210] Exodus 31:3, Judges 14:6, Luke 4:18, Acts 4:8, Acts 9:31, I Corinthians 12)
[211] *Exodus 14*
[212] *II Kings 2:8, 14*
[213] Joshua 6:1-21

feet and backs hurt. It was hot. They were discouraged. Nothing was happening, so what was the point? (Ever said any of these things? I know I have!)

How often do we stop praying because we have not seen the "walls" fall down? How often are we one prayer away from a breakthrough? In truth, you'll never know if you stop praying.

DAILY STORY:

During World War II (1940), over 300,000 Allied soldiers were trapped on the beaches of Dunkirk, surrounded by the German army. Facing certain annihilation, the British monarch, King George VI, called for a National Day of Prayer. On that day, a sudden storm grounded the German Luftwaffe, while "a great calm" settled over the English Channel, allowing a fleet of small civilian boats to successfully evacuate the soldiers in a massive operation. Many historians and people at the time considered this an example of "divine intervention in response to a desperate, final plea." [214] The soldiers could have accepted their fate, but instead, they turned to the Almighty God and He heard their prayers.

---

[214] Robinson, R.C. (2025). Documented prayer throughout history.

Mark 9:23 states it best: "Everything is possible for one who believes." Believe God can do immense miracles in your life. Anticipate big things. Expect endless provision. Dare to dream. Persist in your prayers. Begin to fast. Watch God move.

REFLECTION: Read the scriptures listed above, then reflect on them below. Pick out keywords, verses, and themes. Write down how those might apply to your life.

Write down any big issues in your life that look like a deep ocean that you need to cross or a wall that needs to fall down.

_____

_____

_____

_____

_____

_____

_____

_____

_____

_____

_____

_____

_____

DR. KIM MENDOZA

PRAYER: Lord, you see the issues in my life that feel like walls. Please give me faith to keep going and knock them down. Amen.

WRITE YOUR OWN PRAYER:

_____

_____

_____

_____

_____

_____

_____

_____

_____

_____

_____

_____

_____

_____

_____

TODAY'S CHALLENGE: Drive or walk to the place that needs movement. Walk around place or thing seven times praying. The act of this may seem silly, and it may do nothing, but it is the act of faith that could be powerful.

🔥 DAY 35 🔥

Striking the Match

If you believe, you will receive
whatever you ask for in prayer.
(Matthew 21:22, NIV)

"Take that first step in faith. You don't have to see
the whole staircase, just take the first step."
(Martin Luther King Jr.)

DAILY READING:

Matthew 6:25-34; 14:13-33; Hebrews 11

DAILY THOUGHT:

What if we never struck the match to begin with because we didn't believe it would do anything? We would not have a fire. The fire starts because we believe the match can get it going. How often in our walks do we not strike the match?

In the reading today, there are two miracles:

The first miracle is the feeding of the 5,000.[215] The disciples asked Jesus to send the people away. They didn't visualize the miracle. They said, "We have ONLY five loaves and two fish." How often do we approach God the same way? *Lord, I don't have this. I don't have that.* It's not enough. As my sister used to sing as a kid, "Oh, woe is me, I might as well eat some worms."

We need to approach God with boldness and belief, trusting God with everything we're going through. The present and the future are both in God's hands. For the disciples to feed everyone, they had to bring the fish and loaves to Jesus. It wasn't much, but it was enough. The Lord can turn our tiny offering into so much more, but it starts when we hand Him what we do have.

There is not a problem you are facing today that God cannot overcome. We cannot worry and trust God at

---

[215] Matthew 14:13-21

the same time. One cancels the other out. We either trust Him, or we don't.

The second lesson on miracles is the "walking on water."[216] The lesson is about "stepping out." If we stop worrying and trust God, then the next step is a *literal* step. People always say, "Jesus was perfect, He walked on water." Those people forget that Peter walked on water, too. Sure, only for a mere few seconds, but he still stepped out of the boat, and for a moment while he kept his eyes on Jesus, he walked on water.[217]

DAILY STORY:

At one point, my youngest son and his wife gave up everything and came to live with us in order to spend time seeking the face of God. They fasted, they prayed, they humbled themselves before His throne. Sure, there were moments of discouragement, but the Holy Spirit kept saying, "Trust me."

---

[216] Matthew 14:22-33
[217] Matthew 14:29

One day, they felt a strong urge to attend a huge event in Washington, D.C. They packed their car and drove off halfway across the country, with little money in their pockets, completely resting their lives in the Lord's hands, and out of 40,000 people that attended this event, this couple made an impression on the organizers of the event. They were invited to travel to the headquarters a few states over.

So, as my son and his wife did what they always do— they prayed. Specifically, that if that was God's will, they'd be given a *vision*, a *word*, and *free lodging*. First, the *vision*. My son had a vivid dream one night of a black dog fence. When they looked up the headquarters online, wouldn't you know it, there was the same black dog fence. Second, the *word*. During the event, several people who did not know them, knew things about them and told them what was going to happen. Third, free lodging. When the event was over, they still had two weeks before they could go to the headquarters. There was no way they could pay for a place to stay. But God sent some who offered a home for two weeks free of charge.

They may have left my house for an event, but they found their calling. There is no paycheck, but these homeland missionaries trust the God who continues to provide for them daily, weekly, and monthly. They have always had a place to stay since they left. In fact, God gave them $1,500 in two days so they could put a down payment on an apartment.

I love their testimony, because it reminds me about what happens when we are faithful. When we pray. When we trust. When we believe. But most importantly, when we are willing to take a step of faith. God honors faithful trust. I have heard testimony after testimony about how God rewards steps of faith.

Write that check. Take that job. Start that ministry. If you are truly not worried, and you trust God, the next step should be easy.

REFLECTION: Read the scriptures listed above, then reflect on them below. Pick out keywords, verses, and themes. Write down how those might apply to your life.

Take a moment to ask yourself, how could you pray differently? What step of faith might you take?

_____

_____

_____

_____

_____

_____

_____

_____

_____

_____

_____

_____

_____

_____

PRAYER: Lord, help me to trust you when life is scary or chaotic. Give me boldness to do as you are calling me to. Amen.

WRITE YOUR OWN PRAYER:

_____

_____

_____

_____

_____

_____

_____

_____

_____

_____

_____

_____

_____

_____

_____

TODAY'S CHALLENGE: Write that check. Apply for that job. Talk to that person. Just like the faith you exhibited when we talked about purpose, now use the same faith to step out of the boat.

♨ DAY 36 ♨

Seeking the Warmth

Seek the LORD and his strength.
seek His presence continually!
(I Chronicles 16:11, NIV).

"We pray when there's nothing
else we can do,
but God wants us to pray
before we do anything at all."
(Oswald Chambers,
Author of *His Utmost for His Highest*)

DAILY READING:

I Chronicles 28:9-10; Matthew 7:7-8; Exodus 33

DAILY THOUGHT:

If we are shivering in our tent, and there is a campfire lit outside, we might want to seek the warmth of the fire. If we walk to it, the heat will fill and blanket us in warmth. As we seek Christ, the Bible says we will be filled.[218]

Did you ever play hide-and-seek as a kid? I loved playing with the neighborhood kids. We would play for hours. I wanted to hide, but occasionally I had to seek. I have never liked losing, so when I was the seeker, I sought hard. I didn't want anyone getting to base on my watch. If you are seeking something, you are not sitting down. You are not resting. You are not going in the opposite direction. You are in transit to the thing you are trying to find. It is a continual process. Seeking is a conscious choice. What does it mean to earnestly seek the Lord? It means the same thing—we're *actively* moving towards Him.

The Bible says as we seek after God, and things of God, they will be found (i.e., all will be added unto

---

[218] Jeremiah 29:13

us). [219] If you want a bountiful life with goodness overflowing, you have to pursue the Savior first, above all. We make Him the *first* priority in our lives. The reality is, the more we do this, all those things that will be "added unto us," won't matter as much any longer.

DAILY STORY:

I met Lee Strobel once at a writer's conference (he probably wouldn't remember me, but I remember him). After meeting him, I read his book, *The Case for Christ.* (If you haven't read it, I highly recommend it.) Lee was a self-proclaimed atheist, when his wife found Christ.[220] In an effort to disprove Christianity and get his wife back, Lee pursued the *historical* Jesus. Or should I say, sought to "disprove" Christianity. At the time, he worked as an investigative journalist for the *Chicago Tribune.* Using his skills, he researched the evidence. What he discovered was that Jesus Christ was who He said He was, that the resurrection was real, and that he needed to give his life over to the Messiah. This decision led him to quit his swanky high-profile

---

[219] Matthew 6:33

[220] Harmon, J. (n.d.) Interview with Lee Strobel. Side B Stories, Episode. 80.

job at the paper to go into ministry. I'm sure people thought he was nuts, but when we find Jesus, nothing else should matter.

If you want to test your spiritual depth, your love for Jesus—consider this. God tells Moses to go ahead and take the land flowing with milk and honey, but He will not be going with him.[221] And Moses' response is, if you're not going, God, I'm not going.[222] Think of your dreams, your prayer requests, and all the things you own. If I said to you, you could have everything you have ever prayed for, but God's presence will not go with you, would you take the deal?

The easy answer is, "No, of course not." But slow down and reflect. What if your mother was dying of cancer and you want her to be healed? What if you really needed to sell your home because the mortgage is hurting your bottom line? What if your kid has terrible anxiety, and you are praying for a cure? What

---

[221] Exodus 33:3
[222] Exodus 33:15

if the perfect job just opened up and they want to hire you?

Now, what if God said to you, "I will give you all those things you've been praying for, but after that, I will no longer be with you." Would you still agree? Or would you say I will live with the outcome, but Jesus, I need you. It is saying, "The Lord may not cure my mom, but I trust He knows what's best." It declares, "My house will sell when it is time, and until then Jesus will supply our needs." It understands that God's grace is sufficient, even when our kid is hurting. It is being able to turn down that perfect job when God tells you it isn't a good fit.

Of course, we know Jesus will never leave or forsake us, but nothing can stand between the Lord and our relationship to Him. I believe this is why Jesus asked, "'Who is my mother, and who are my brothers?' Pointing to his disciples, he said, 'Here are my mother and my brothers. For whoever does the will of my Father in heaven is my brother and sister and mother.'"[223] It is about making Him number one in our lives, and the truth is, as we pursue God, our concerns, dreams, and desires will change. Our hearts begin to care less about the world around us, and more about Kingdom aspirations.

---

[223] Matthew 12:48-50

REFLECTION: Read the scriptures listed above, then reflect on them below. Pick out keywords, verses, and themes. Write down how those might apply to your life.

Reflect on the question stated above. Could you get all your prayers answered, if it meant God would never been your life again. The answer tells you which is more important.

_____

_____

_____

_____

_____

_____

_____

_____

_____

_____

_____

_____

_____

_____

Matchbook

PRAYER: Lord, help me to truly seek you in all that I do, all that I am, and all that I am to become. Be what I desire above all else. Amen.

WRITE YOUR OWN PRAYER:

_____

_____

_____

_____

_____

_____

_____

_____

_____

_____

_____

_____

_____

_____

_____

_____

TODAY'S CHALLENGE: Today, shut out all technology, except the ability to listen worship music, and sit in God's presence, seeking the face of Jesus.

🔥 DAY 37 🔥

Feeding the Fire

So, I say, walk by the Spirit, and you will not gratify the desires of the flesh. For the flesh desires what is contrary to the Spirit, and the Spirit what is contrary to the flesh. They are in conflict with each other, so that you are not to do whatever you want.
(Galatians 5:16-17, NIV)

"Those who operate in the Holy Spirit
are more equipped to resist temptation."
(Monica Johnson, Inspirational Speaker)

DAILY READING:

Galatians 5:13-23; *Matthew 3:11; I Corinthians 12:13; John 20:19; Acts 1:14, 2*

DAILY THOUGHT:

As I mentioned early on, if you don't feed your fire, it will eventually go out. But in contrast, if you feed your fire abundantly, it has the ability to light the way for a considerable distance.

There are only a few days left of this challenge. How are you doing? Are you still drawn to worldly things or are you starting to embrace godliness? Walking in the Spirit is a daily choice. We choose what we want to feed our soul. The Bible tells us to avoid the acts of the flesh, and embrace the fruits (love, joy, peace, patience, kindness, goodness, faithfulness, gentleness, and self-control) and people will know us by those fruits.[224] Are you cultivating these fruits into your life? You will find that the more time you spend with God, the easier these are. We become less argumentative and anxious. We find joy and peace in all situations. We desire to be good and kind. God gives us the ability to reach self-control. And ultimately, we love more, as God is love.

---

[224] Galations 5:22-23; Matthew 7:16

DAILY STORY:

When I was in high school, one of my youth leaders fell on an ice rink and was pronounced brain dead. Even though his mind no longer functioned, his mouth sang worship songs. The doctors had no explanation. But I did. The music we hear feeds our spirit. It wasn't his mind singing (that was dead), but his soul. What are you feeding your soul? Whatever is going in will ultimately come out.

As we mentioned early on, people often consider their physical bodies and their mental health but ignore the spiritual condition. What are we feeding our spirits? What voice is speaking into our souls? This happens not just with music, but television, social media, movies, and video games. Christians love to say, "That's my guilty pleasure," as if that excuses our behavior. But we have a higher calling.[225] Sure, some of those "guilty pleasures" won't send us to hell, but they do not nurture our spirits either.

---

[225] Romans 12:2; I Peter 2:9; Ephesians 4:23-24; Deuteronomy 7:6

Besides getting on fire for the Lord, this forty-day journey is meant to produce more spiritual fruit in your life. To put a spotlight on anything that might prevent you from being the best version of yourself. What are you feeding your soul?

REFLECTION: Read the scriptures listed above, then reflect on them below. Pick out keywords, verses, and themes. Write down how those might apply to your life.

Write down the different fruits and evaluate how present they are in your life. Think about your habits. Is there anything else that is harmful to your walk?

_____

_____

_____

_____

_____

_____

_____

_____

_____

_____

_____

_____

_____

Matchbook

PRAYER: Holy Spirit come and help me do the Lord's will. Help me get rid of anything that hinders my walk with you. Amen.

WRITE YOUR OWN PRAYER:

_____

_____

_____

_____

_____

_____

_____

_____

_____

_____

_____

_____

_____

_____

TODAY'S CHALLENGE: What are you feeding your soul? Your challenge today is committing to eliminate anything destructive in your life. It can be symbolic; it can be literal. That is between you and God.

♨ DAY 38 ♨

Valuing the Coals

But when you pray, go into your room and shut the door and pray to your Father who is in secret. And your Father who sees in secret will reward you.
(Matthew 6:6, NIV)

"God speaks in the silence of the heart.
Listening is the beginning of prayer."
(Mother Teresa)

DAILY READING: Mark 1:35; 6:45-46; Luke 5:16; Ephesians 6:18; I Thessalonians 5:17

DAILY THOUGHT:

When a fire first starts, it is loud. The crackle, pop, and sizzle can be deafening, especially if there are things in the pit that do not belong there (i.e., plastics, chemicals, or trash). But as the fire burns, it starts to calm. The noisy, frantic flames subside, allowing the heat to fuse into a deep, silent bed of coals. When this happens, it is nice to be alone in the quiet, to relish the fire.

Over and over in Scripture, we see that Jesus withdrew to pray. [226] He understood the importance of time spent with only the Father. In this challenge, you have ventured to spend quality time with God, but this needs to be a long-term commitment—a lifestyle. The distractions of this fallen world can be deafening. They divert our focus and draw us in. If we're not careful, before we realize it, our faith has diminished.

One of the challenge groups I worked with a few years ago mentioned how the time in silence revealed a lot of issues in their lives—things they thought they had dealt with. Those private moments with God can be like a spiritual mirror, a true reflection of our walk. As Jesus modeled, we need to withdraw and have time to hear from our Savior.

---

[226] Matthew 14:23; Luke 5:16; Mark 1:35, 6:46

DAILY STORY:

I have completed this challenge four times. Every time I do it, God reveals to me new ministry opportunities, cleans out more of my issues, and helps me yield a better life. This last time, He showed me bitterness I harbored that I didn't even realize was there. This might seem silly, but I was bitter that I had to ask my husband to take out the trash. Often there'd be a bunch of bags, and it smelled in the kitchen. But the more time I spent with Jesus, the more I had to admit the bitterness existed.

One day, my son suggested I take out the trash myself. My first inclination was, "Absolutely not. I'm not doing that. He should have to..." Blah, blah, blah. My heart was so black to this idea, I dug in my heels and refused. But my son challenged me (as I have challenged you) to pray about it. So, with disdain (being fully transparent here), I brought the matter before the Lord. He agreed with my son. The Holy Spirit showed me the deep-rooted bitterness. He also showed me where the freedom would be found—from taking out the trash. As soon as I obeyed in this way, the bitterness was lifted.

The reason this challenge works is because it decreases distractions and directs our hearts back to the Lord. It gives the Holy Spirit a chance to speak into our lives—to reveal the pains, the hurts, the bitterness, the sin, and the shadows of our former lives that have informed our way of living. It is in the silence that the soft whisper of the Holy Spirit can be heard. I likened it to a Discipleship and Ministry Training (DMT)* in book form.

*A foundational Christian program that is designed to draw a person away from the world so he or she can be closer to God. The traditional DMT calls a person to a center anywhere in the world from twelve weeks to a year. Examples of organizations that offer these intensive programs include Awaken the Dawn University (ATDU), Master's Commission, Teen Challenge, and Youth with a Mission (YWAM).

REFLECTION: Read the scriptures listed above, then reflect on them below. Pick out keywords, verses, and themes. Write down how those might apply to your life.

Consider what you will do when these 40 days are over. What, where, when, and how will you continue to seek Him?

_____

_____

_____

_____

_____

_____

_____

_____

_____

_____

_____

_____

_____

_____

PRAYER: Holy Spirit come and anoint me, allowing me to do the Lord's will. Amen.

WRITE YOUR OWN PRAYER:

_____

_____

_____

_____

_____

_____

_____

_____

_____

_____

_____

_____

_____

_____

_____

_____

_____

_____

TODAY'S CHALLENGE: Get away from everything and everyone. Tarry with the Lord for one hour. Meditate on His Word. Speak out loud. Journal your emotions. Cry on His shoulder. Wait for His response.

⚶ DAY 39 ⚶

Safeguarding the Ring

Beloved, do not believe every spirit, but test the
spirits to see whether they are from God, for many
false prophets have gone out into the world.
(I John 4:1, NIV)

"It's been said that only the educated are free, but I
contend. Only those who are educated with TRUTH
can be inherently free. Otherwise, you are simply
indoctrinated with error."
(J.E.B. Spredemann, *Amish Author*)

DAILY READING:
Jude 1; II Corinthians 11:1-15

DAILY THOUGHT:
The fire ring is where our fire grows safely. Today, our
metaphor of the "fire ring" is the Christian church and

the "flames" are the true Gospel of Jesus Christ. Our message must be contained within the Word of God. If a spark gets out of the fire ring, it can grow into a raging fire that is destructive. This is why we guard the flames like "watchmen" [227] and put out any stray embers. The Bible states that we shouldn't sleep but be watchful, keeping awake and sober. [228] In today's society, we have a front row seat to this warping of the Gospel to fit certain needs and aspirations. Little sparks of truth are taken out of context and grow into destructive forces in our faith, leading thousands of people astray. This is not another lesson on just reading your Bible every day. A lot of Christians do that. No, this is a lesson on going <u>deeper</u>.

Since the phenomenon of YouTube, a lot of false prophets and heretical preachers have become popular, spewing messages that are contrary to the Word of God. We shouldn't be surprised, as Jesus, Peter, and Paul, all stated this would happen. [229] These people take one verse out of context, and design

---

[227] Ezekiel 33:6
[228] I Thessalonians 5:6; Colossians 4:2
[229] Matthew 24:11; II Peter 2:1; II Timothy 4:3

entire theologies based on that one sentence. The problem is that scripture is made up of context, depth, and reoccurrence. To truly understand scripture, surface reading is incomplete. There are historical and cultural events happening in Paul's letters. There are threads that point back to the Old Testament and New Testament. Did you know that Daniel points to Revelation?[230] That the Psalms are full of Messianic prophecy?[231] That the Messiah coming is mentioned in Genesis? [232] In truth, to fully understand the New Testament, we must study the Old Testament. To fully grasp the context, we need to study biblical history and ancient Jewish culture.

More than ever, it is essential to know what God said. As evangelist, Christine Caine preached: "If you don't know what God really said, then you will believe what the enemy said."[233] We need to be suspicious of any man who states something that does not line up with,

---

[230] Example: Daniel 12:7 & Revelation 12:14

[231] Example: Psalm 22

[232] Genesis 3:15

[233] Caine, C. (2018). Did God really say? Seacoast Church. Sermon.

(or tries to tweak) God's Word. But in order to do this, we must know what it says for ourselves.

We have an all-access pass to the King of Kings' personal journal. The Bible was written to reveal the Creator. To show us how to live. Above all, to speak Truth. If something doesn't sound right, question it, research it (not from man, but from God), and determine if it lines up with the Scripture.

DAILY STORY:

My real father grew up in the church. He taught Sunday School and attended Bible college. But before he died, he said, "I don't believe Jesus is the Christ." I discovered, he hated everything about Christianity. So, how does one get from attending Bible college to despising Jesus on their deathbed? By believing a lie. My dad sought "spiritual truth" for years. He didn't want his beliefs to just be his parent's beliefs. So, he traveled from church to church, denomination to denomination asking questions. During his spiritual quest, he met a man who fed him false doctrine, and it stuck. The reason? My dad was a textbook narcissist, and what he really sought was a belief that allowed him the power to control *his own* destiny. His pursuit did not end until he found that false narrative.

This false narrative from the enemy has been going on since Creation in the Garden when the serpent asked, "Did God really say...?" and "You will certainly not die..." and "God knows...your eyes will be opened..." and "You will be like God..."[234] The enemy has worked on distorting Truth since the start. John 8:44 states: "...he was a murderer from the beginning, not holding to truth, for there is no truth in him. When he lies, he speaks his native language, for he is a liar and the father of lies." The father of lies. That is how the devil operates. You want truth, you must seek God alone. Jesus said, "*I AM* the Way, **TRUTH**, and Life."[235] Truth must dictate every area of our lives. In order to know Truth, it is essential to know what the Creator of Truth, and we discover Him in the God-breathed Word of God.

---

[234] Genesis 3:1-4
[235] John 14:6

Everything we believe and do must line up with Scripture.[236] Throughout this challenge, I have cited the Bible in the footnotes. This was not simply to back up my words, but so you could read the scriptures in context. It is important that we never follow mankind before God.

As you draw to an end of this challenge, the enemy will try to snuff out your fire. His lies are like retardant over the flames of our spiritual walks. If we listen to the lies, they can smother our fervor for Christ and choke out the good He's doing in our lives. On the other hand, God's truth is like a blast of lighter fluid on the flames. It burns up the dross (the rubbish) and instantly incinerates the enemy's deceit to ash.

---

[236] Colossians 3:17; I John 2:3-4

REFLECTION: Read the scriptures listed above, then reflect on them below. Pick out keywords, verses, and themes. Write down how those might apply to your life.

In your own words, write how you personally know when something lines up with Truth. Have you ever found yourself following a minister or ministry without ever questioning if the teaching is in line with God's Word?

_____

_____

_____

_____

_____

_____

_____

_____

_____

_____

_____

_____

Matchbook

PRAYER: Lord, help me to discern Truth. Let me be hungry for your words and bring them to me when needed. Amen.

WRITE YOUR OWN PRAYER:

_____

_____

_____

_____

_____

_____

_____

_____

_____

_____

_____

_____

_____

_____

_____

_____

_____

TODAY'S CHALLENGE: Take a hard look at the people you allow to speak into your life. Are they solid in the faith, speaking Truth? If not, I challenge you to stop listening. Stop going. Turning the channel.

🔥 DAY 40 🔥

Walking in Blue Fire Faith

But seek first the kingdom of
God and his righteousness,
and all these things will be added to you.
(Matthew 6:33, NIV)

"Prayer is not an appointment; it is a lifestyle."
(Kimberlee Mendoza, *Blue Fire Faith* Vlog)

DAILY READING:

II Timothy 6:11-21; James 1:22-27

DAILY THOUGHT:

One of the hottest fires is blue. It ranges between

1,800—2,400 degrees Fahrenheit.[237] Blue flames are typically seen in the cleanest of fires.

So, we made it—Day 40! How blue is your fire?

I remember completing this challenge with a group who said they were afraid of Day 41. Fearful that they would go back to the way it was before. On Day 1, I spoke about getting in shape and starting a diet. After forty days of hard work at the gym and a healthy diet, you wouldn't want to throw it all away by binging and quitting—all the pain and sweat would have been for nothing. The same is true with our spiritual selves. It is time to live a godly life. As my quote states above, this is the new lifestyle.

DAILY STORY:

In the early 1940's, Reverend Dietrich Bonhoeffer opposed the Nazi takeover of Germany, refusing to allow anyone to preach heresy. His resistance eventually led to his execution. Most theologians

---

[237] Helmenstine, A.M. (2024). Flame temperatures table for different fuels. *Thought Co.*

deem him a hero for the Christian faith. During his time in prison, he wrote many writings that still influence the church today: "We must be ready to allow ourselves to be interrupted by God... If you seek God alone, you will gain happiness... One act of obedience is worth a hundred sermons."[238] This new lifestyle comes from understanding what Bonhoeffer was trying to say. Are you ready for where God might take you? You must seek Him and obey His calling. Only then will you be able to walk in this new lifestyle.

Here are some tips:

1. **Buy a devotional and/or a One-Year Bible.**

    These will help you keep on track and continue to seek Him regularly. I recommend the Two-Year Bible, as it is easier to digest. If you need a devotional recommendation, seek out your pastor, check out reviews online, or see my list at the end.

---

[238] Wood, E.M. (n.d,) 15 inspiring Dietrich Bonhoffer quotes. Crosswalk.

2. **Buy a new journal to keep writing down your prayers and struggles with God.**

   I think a new journal makes the next step feel like a fresh journey.

3. **Keep this book handy—when in doubt, remember what you did in this challenge.**

   I often return to old journals to remind myself of what God has brought me through. A good reminder of this time can spark a new perspective or remind you of an old one.

4. **Maintain your schedule.**

   Whatever time you marked out for God during these forty days, keep it going. That consistency will help you be successful going forward.

5. **Don't introduce those distractions back into your life.**

   You worked so hard to get rid of those disruptions that weren't good for you, why bring them back? If you dieted and lost fifty pounds, would you start eating junk food the next day?

6. **Find an accountability partner, if you don't have one already.**

>   If you don't already have one, get someone who can speak into your life. Be like Paul and have a Barnabas and a Timothy (someone who mentors you and someone you mentor).

7. **Get involved in ministry.**

>   Ministry keeps you accountable and gives you a chance to serve the church body and Jesus. It is harder to falter when you know you are responsible to others in the church. If you're really hungry for more, see the list of information in the appendix on DTMs.

REFLECTION: Read the scriptures listed above, then reflect on them below. Pick out keywords, verses, and themes. Write down how those might apply to your life.

Reflect this week on the last 40 days and write where you are at. Consider if you could have all your requests granted, but God's presence will not go with you any longer, would you take the deal?

_____

_____

_____

_____

_____

_____

_____

_____

_____

_____

_____

_____

_____

PRAYER: Dear Lord, as I end my forty-day journey, I pray that I have the strength to continue to grow and draw closer to you. Amen.

WRITE YOUR OWN PRAYER:

_____

_____

_____

_____

_____

_____

_____

_____

_____

_____

_____

_____

_____

_____

_____

_____

TODAY'S CHALLENGE: Do 1-7 above! May you be on fire and light your city up! Be blessed!

Check out @BlueFireFaith on YouTube.

www.kimmendoza.com

RECOMMENDATIONS TO KEEP THE FIRE BURNING

DAILY DEVOTIONALS:

Experiencing the Heart of Jesus for 52 Weeks by Max Lucado

God's Purpose for Your Life by Charles F. Stanley

Praying the Names of God by Ann Spangler

The Two-Year Bible by Tyndale

Truth for Each Day by Billy Graham

Wisdom for Today by Chuck Smith

OTHER BOOKS WORTH READING:

A Praying Life by Paul E. Miller

Prayer that Ignites Revival by Joe Oden

Sitting at the Feet of Rabbi Jesus by Spangler & Tverberg

The Case for Christ by Lee Strobel

The Cross & the Switchblade by David Wilkerson

The Greatest Power in the World by Kathryn Kuhlman

CLASSICS WORTH READING:

Knowing God by J.I. Packer

Mere Christianity by C.S. Lewis

My Utmost for His Highest by Oswald Chambers

The Pursuit of God by A.W. Tozer

The Cost of Discipleship by Dietrich Bonhoeffer

DISCIPLESHIP AND MINISTRY TRAINING

Awaken the Dawn University

ATDU combines sound biblical training with experiential Holy Spirit living in the context of vibrant community and now includes the ability to receive college credit through Faith University. ATDU exists to serve you as you are discovering your calling and assignment!

Website: https://awakenthedawn.com/atdu/

Global University

Global University's School for Evangelism and Discipleship provides you with the training to deepen your faith and encouragement to share your faith with others.

https://globaluniversity.edu/sed/

Master's Commission

The collective vision of Master's Commission is to know God and make Him known. This vision takes unique shape in each of our individual programs. As a network of Master's Commissions our vision is to see Jesus' model of discipleship spread throughout the globe.

Website: http://mcin.org/

Teen Challenge USA (for both Adults & Teens)

A life-changing residential program that gives people the chance to start over, become a new person, live a godly life, and find freedom from life style choices and addictions through a restored purpose and an eternal hope. We do this through classes, individual study, personal mentoring, work ethics training, and involvement in the Christian community.
Website: https://teenchallengeusa.org/about/

YWAM

The program gives you an opportunity to discover your passions and your part in God's purposes for the world. It is for those who long to follow Jesus in new ways with a different perspective.
Website: https://ywam.org/dts

School of Discipleship

To develop Christ-like character, integrity and maturity in people, preparing them for positions of responsible spiritual influence and leadership. At the same time, this program also provides practical training and experience in a variety of skill areas within the Christian camping ministry.
Website: https://schoolofdiscipleship.org/about/

OTHER BOOKS BY KIMBERLEE R. MENDOZA

NONFICTION BOOKS
- *Torrid Faith: Forty-day Faith Challenge for Teens*
- *Teaching Squirrels: How to Reach Generation Z*
- *The Human Video Handbook*
- *Level Up: Gaining Skills to Write*

CHRISTIAN FICTION
- *Torn Slipper: A Backwards Cinderella Story*
- *Confessions of a Con Man*
- *Dark Cognitions*
- *Reveille of the Heart*
- *Taps to the Soul*
- *The Seraph War*

YOUNG ADULT FICTION
- *The Forgotten Ones*
- *The Lost Few*
- *The Hidden Two*
- *Love thy Sister, Guard thy Man*
- *Oh Brother, You're Not My Keeper*
- *Seek Ye First*

NOVELLAS
- *A Girl Named Christmas*
- *Lilly's Garden, an Easter Tale*
- *Johnny B. Goode for Christmas*
- *The Seraph War*
- *Unchartered Waters*

PLAYS

Go to: https://www.christianpub.com [search *Mendoza]*

REFERENCES

Batterson, M. (2016). Circle maker: Praying circles around your biggest dreams and greatest fears. Zondervan

Beck, P. (2010). The voice of faith: Jonathan Edward's theology of prayer. Sola Scriptura Ministries International.

Bennett, R. T. (2021). The Light in the Heart. Independently Published.

Bouchet, et al. (2020). Baby cry recognition is independent of motherhood but improved by experience and exposure. The Royal Society of Publishing. Retrieved from https://pmc.ncbi.nlm.nih.gov/articles/PMC7062011/

Brissette, C. (2018). This is your body on fast food. The Washington Post. Retrieved from https://www.washingtonpost.com/lifestyle/wellness/sneaking-a-little-junk-food-doesnt-mean-all-is-lost/2018/02/26/828b75fa-1b36-11e8-9de1-147dd2df3829_story.html

Caine, C. (2018). Did God really say? Seacoast Church. Sermon. YouTube. Retrieved from https://youtu.be/sd3B7k1TNqA?si=BnoFMxe8QJ9yq2HY

Carter, J. (n.d.) Attributed. (on various sites: Brainy Quote, BibleinSong, Famous Quotes, etc.)

Catherine of Sienna. (1376). Letter. UC Davis. Retrieved from https://medieval.ucdavis.edu/20C/Catherine.html

Caviezel, J. (2024). "I was struck by lightning." TBN. Facebook. Retrieved from https://www.facebook.com/share/v/17dyb4LZD4/

Chadwick, S. (1932). The way to Pentecost. CLC Publications.

Chambers, O. (1927). His Utmost for His Highest. Simpkin, Marshall, Hamilton, Kent, & Co.

Chesterton, G.K. (as cited by The Christian Post. "The courage, creativity and charm of GK Chesterton, 2021). Retrieved from https://www.christianpost.com/voices/the-courage-creativity-and-charm-of-gk-chesterton.html

Diepenbrock, G. (2015). Book traces origin of phrase in WWJD movement to Topeka minister. KU News. https://news.ku.edu/news/article/2015/04/24/book-traces-origin-phrase-wwjd-movement-topeka-minister-social-activistEarls, A. (2019). How often do you read the Bible. Lifeway Research. Retrieved from https://research.lifeway.com/2019/07/02/few-protestant-churchgoers-read-the-bible-daily/#:~:text=Evangelical%20Protestants%20(36%25)%20and,they%20read%20Scripture%20every%20day

Edelman, MW. (1986). Interview. Cleveland Plain Dealer.

Ford, H. (1922). My life and work. Doubleday, Page, & Company

Gambino, L. (2025). Erika Kirk, Charlie Kirk's widow, says she forgives the man accused of murder. The Guardian. Retrieved from https://www.theguardian.com/us-news/2025/sep/21/erika-kirk-charlie-kirk-killing

Global Teen Challenge. Until all live free. Retrieved from https://globaltc.org/global-locations/

Glor, J. (2013, December 12). Mother of Amish school shooter shares amazing story of forgiveness. CBS News. https://www.cbsnews.com/news/mother-of-amish-school-shooter-shares-amazing-story-of-forgiveness/

Graham, B. (2021). Why should I read the Bible? Billy Graham Evangelistic Association. Retrieved from https://billygraham.org/articles/why-should-i-read-the-bible

Graham, B. (n.d.). "I'm a new Christian trying to clean up my language." Billy Graham Evangelistic Association. Retrieved from https://billygraham.org/answers/im-a-new-christian-trying-to-clean-up-my-language-whats-the-best-way-to-do-this

Grosset, S. (2020). Five good reasons to trust God's timing. Daily She. Retrieved from https://dailyshepursues.com/reasons-to-trust-gods-timing/

Hagin, Kenneth. (n.d). Bible Study Course. Goodreads. Retrieved from https://www.goodreads.com/quotes/7293129-the-bible-says-it-i-believe-it-and-that-settles

Harmon, J. (n.d.) Interview with Lee Strobel. Side B Stories, Episode. 80. Retrieved from https://www.cslewisinstitute.org/resources/the-side-b-stories-lee-strobel/

Helmenstine, A.M. (2024). Flame temperatures table for different fuels. Thought Co. Retrieved from https://www.thoughtco.com/flame-temperatures-table-607307

Huie, J.L. (2008). Regrets, Resentments and the Path to Forgiveness - Stop Anger & Live Happy With Conscious Awareness. Jonathan Lockwood Huie's Daily Inspiration. Retrieved from https://old.jlhuie.com/2008/11/regrets-resentments-and-path-to.html Attributed (on various sites: Psychology Today, Good Reads, San Diego State University, etc.)

Hunt, T.W. (2008). The Mind of Christ, Revised. Lifeway Press.

Israel Team. (n.d.) The Arab people have a unique and special calling. Israel Team Blog. Retrieved from https://www.israelteam.org/issues/special-calling-of-the-arab-people/

Jacobson, S. (2023). The real story of Ismael: What they don't tell you. Meaning Life Center. YouTube. Retrieved from https://www.youtube.com/watch?v=_sFjLwA4qt0

Jerimiah, D. (2013). The Jeremiah study Bible: What it says, what it means. Worthy Books.

Johnson, M. (as cited by everydaypower.com)

Kolby, K. (n.d.) Jesus was scourged: The Roman flagrum. Thirty-Three Ministries. Retrieved from https://threethirtyministries.com/the-roman-flagrum/

Lucado, M. (2007). Grace for the moment. Volume I, Inspirational Thoughts for Each Day of the Year. Thomas Nelson.

"Lupus." (2022). The Mayo Clinic. Retrieved from https://www.mayoclinic.org/diseases-conditions/lupus/symptoms-causes/syc-20365789

Luther, M. (1546). Letter to his wife.

Marina, M. (2023). Crucifixion in the Roman world: Ideology behind the brutal practice. HI(S)TORY. Retrieved from https://tragoviproslosti.eu/2023/05/09/crucifixion-in-the-roman-world-ideology-behind-the-brutal-practice/

Moody, D.L. (as cited in Gospel Academy on Word Press, 2016). Retrieved from https://wetrainchristians.wordpress.com/2016/07/18/inspiring-quote-by-d-l-moody/

Mote, E. (1834). Hymns of Praise, A New Selection of Gospel Hymns. J. Nichols. London.

Murakami, H. (2006). Kafka on the shore. Vintage Publisher.

National Geographic Society. (n.d.). Ants. National Geographic. Retrieved August 8, 2025, from https://www.nationalgeographic.com/animals/invertebrates/facts/ants

Nee, Watchman. (1968). The spiritual man. Christian Fellowship Publishers.

Nevid, J. S. (2024). The psychological power of words. Psychology Today. Retrieved from https://www.psychologytoday.com/us/blog/the-minute-therapist/202407/the-psychological-power-of-words

Nicolotti, A. (2017). The scourge of Jesus and the Roman scourge. Journal for the Study of the Historical Jesus. 1-59. Retrieved from https://www.scribd.com/document/471768419/Journal-for-the-Study-of-the-Historical-Jesus-15-2017-James-G-Crossley-Anthony-Le-Donne-eds-1

Omartian, S. (2013). The 7-day prayer warrior experience. Harvest House Publishers.

Packer, J.I. (1973). Knowing God. Intervarsity Press.

Pierson, A.T. (as cited in Arthur Wallis' book, In the Day of Power, 2010, Clc Publishers.)

Reich, R. (2019). Wedging vs. kneading. Ceramic Arts Network. Retrieved here https://community.ceramicartsdaily.org/topic/19981-wedging-vs-kneading/

Robinson, R.C. (2025). Documented prayer throughout history. Robert Clifton Robinson. Retrieved from https://robertcliftonrobinson.com/2025/01/11/documented-prayer-throughout-history/#:~:text=1.,2.

Roosevelt, T. (as cited on TeddyRoosevelt.com, "Theodore Roosevelt and Religion,"2014). Retrieved from https://teddyrooseveltlive.com/2014/04/19/theodore-roosevelt-and-religion/

Sauter, M. (2025). The church of Laodicea in the Bible and archaeology. Biblical Archaeology Society. Retrieved from https://www.biblicalarchaeology.org/daily/biblical-sites-places/biblical-archaeology-sites/church-of-laodicea-in-the-bible-and-archaeology/

Silliman, D. (2023). No celebrities except Jesus: How Asbury protected the revival. Christianity Today. Retrieved from https://www.christianitytoday.com/2023/02/asbury-revival-outpouring-protect-work-admin-volunteers/

Simpson, Sandy. (n.d.). The real heretical teachings of Kenneth Hagin. Grace Panorama. Retrieved from https://www.gracepano.com/language/en/2022/10/17/the-real-heretical-teachingsof-kenneth-hagin/

Sorge, B. (2001). Secrets of the secret place: Keys to igniting your personal time with God. Oasis House.

Smithsonian Institute Archives. (n.d.) Smokey bear. Retrieved from https://siarchives.si.edu/history/featured-topics/pictures/smokey-bear

Spurgeon, C.(1883). All joy in all trials. The Spurgeon Center. Retrieved from https://www.spurgeon.org/resource-library/sermons/all-joy-in-all-trials/#flipbook/

Stanley, C. (2010). I life up my soul: Devotions to start your day with God. Thomas Nelson.

Swindoll, C. (2023). Life is 10% what happens to you and 90% how you react. Thomas Nelson.

ten Boom, C. (1971). The hiding place. Chosen Books.

Tenney, T. (1998). God Chasers. Destiny Image Publishers.

Towey, J. (2022). Mother Teresa and the sisters who stay. Aging with Dignity. Retrieved from https://agingwithdignity.org/mother-teresa-and-the-sisters-who-stay/

Towzer, A.W. (1954). The Christian's strange and fiery trials. Sermon Transcripts. Retrieved from https://tozertalks.com/tozer-talks-102/

Tsarfati, A. (2025). Preach the Gospel. YouTube. Retrieved from https://www.youtube.com/watch?v=4RRWMSAGGU4

Von Buseck, C. (2025).Famous Christian women who change the modern world. Focus on the Family. Retrieved from https://www.focusonthefamily.com/parenting/famous-christian-women-who-changed-the-modern-world/

Warren, R. (2002). The purpose driven life. Zondervan.

Weissman, S. (2023). The aftershocks of the Asbury revival. Inside Higher Ed. Retrieved from https://www.insidehighered.com/news/institutions/religious-colleges/2023/03/01/asbury-revival-comes-close

Whitman, A. (2023). Jesus revolution: The 60s hippies who changed the world. Premier Christianity. Retrieved from https://www.premierchristianity.com/features/jesus-revolution-the-60s-hippies-who-changed-the-world/3787.article

Wilkerson, D. (2008). The Cross & the Switchblade. Berkley Press.

Wood, E.M. (n.d,) 15 inspiring Dietrich Bonhoffer quotes. Crosswalk. Retrieved from: https://www.crosswalk.com/faith/spiritual-life/20-influential-quotes-by-dietrich-bonhoeffer.html?gad_source=1&gad_campaignid=20553081541&gclid=CjOKCQjwo63HBhCKARIsAHOHV_XezWEcA5RyllaxlUhV0KOXnsOkcl85pp1kBK7TgPQySKc_arDNoxkaAsOTEALw_wcB

Woods, R.A. (2012). The journey is the destination: A photo journal. Rhema Rising Press.

Ziglar, Z. (1926). The most powerful lesson. Ziglar. Retrieved from https://www.ziglar.com/articles/the-most-powerful-lesson/

For supplemental sermons, check out
@BlueFireFaith on YouTube.

DR. KIM MENDOZA

www.ingramcontent.com/pod-product-compliance
Lightning Source LLC
LaVergne TN
LVHW041314080426
835513LV00008B/447